NETWORKING FOR DRASTIC RESULTS™

Strategies to Get Known, Get Connected, and Get Paid!

COMPILED BY TONI HARRIS TAYLOR
FOREWORD BY DR. GEORGE C. FRASER

Viral Networking for Drastic Results

Copyright © 2022 by Toni Harris-Taylor

All rights reserved. No part of this book may be reproduced, stored in a retrieval system, or transmitted in any form or by any means—electronic, mechanical, digital, photocopy, or any other—without prior permission from the publisher and author, except as provided by the United States of America copyright law.

For more information visit:

363 N. Sam Houston Parkway East, Suite 1845
Houston, TX 77060

NIAGlobalPartners.com

713.387.9273

Printed in the United States of America

First Trade Edition: September, 2022

Book Production: Marvin D. Cloud

Editor: Joyce Jenkins

I dedicate this book to all the frustrated entrepreneurs who want to go viral with their networking to grow their businesses and get DRASTIC results.

—Toni Harris Taylor

ACKNOWLEDGMENTS

Thank you to all the contributors to this fantastic project, *Viral Networking for Drastic Results,* who shared the good, bad, and ugly of networking for business. Sharing your journey will help another entrepreneur who H-A-T-E-S networking to avoid mistakes and do it right from this point forward.

Thank you to my family, who supports every drastic idea I introduce.

Special thanks to the project team: book expert, Marvin D. Cloud; editor Joyce P. Jenkins, and my virtual assistant and cover designer, Janice Macadenden.

FOREWORD

Networking is the key to success in all relationships and businesses. As the founder of the *Power*Networking Conference and Fraser Nation over the past 21 years, I have had the privilege of bringing together entrepreneurs who have a passion for building connections to expand their businesses and change their lives. Forbes voted our conference one of the top five "can't miss" conferences for entrepreneurs in the world. However, I didn't start out as a power networker. In fact, my journey began with a very humble beginning.

I am from Bed-Stuy, New York. My mother suffered from mental illness, and I was adopted at two years old along with my 11 siblings. My first real job was mopping floors on a midnight shift at LaGuardia Airport for about three years. Today, if you go to LaGuardia Airport, go down into the maintenance department, and there's a big picture on the wall. It's me. I was the best floor mopper and won every award in the history of LaGuardia Airport's maintenance department. What's the point? It's not how you start; it's how you finish. How you do anything is how you do everything. That's where networking comes in. Excellence is what I attempt to model. You must model the behavior that you expect from your network. I don't care what you're doing, what project you're invested in or involved in, do it with excellence or don't do it at all.

In my book, *Click-10 Truths for Building Extraordinary Relationships*, one truth is to be open to everything and attached to nothing. The best idea wins. Even if it isn't your idea. Where do you get the best ideas? You get the best ideas from your network. I am grateful that I discovered at a young age that there is no success that you can attain, sustain, or maintain on your own by yourself. in a vacuum. If you cannot do it with or through other people, you're just not going to achieve what you envision. The way to reach your goals is with and through human connections. Why? So that they can serve us, and we can serve them. It is critical to understand the value and importance of creating a strong network. There are approximately 1.3 million people in my network. I've built my reputation and trust in a large body of people that are ready to serve and be served.

Why was money created? Money was created as the primary incentive for you to serve. I like to call money, certificates of appreciation. The more skills you have, and the better you serve, the more money you make. If you are not constantly reinventing yourself and building on your skills, you will not make a lot of money. The money you make is in proportion to the number of people you serve. When you think about it, money will incentivize you to develop your skills and serve other people. Networking is the gateway to serving other people. When you're intentional about serving, it comes back to you exponentially in money and relationships.

Toni Harris Taylor is a great example of how to maximize relationships. I've watched Toni grow as a business owner. Toni is networking personified. I've admired how she has taken networking and purchased a

Network in Action franchise to help connect entrepreneurs around the world. She is doing exactly what I teach my conference attendees; build relationships and create connections to serve others. She teaches her clients how to take their business viral with simple networking strategies that work. In this Viral Networking book, Toni brought together entrepreneurs who are willing to share their networking experiences. Practice the strategies you read, cultivate relationships, and start collecting more certificates of appreciation and you will win.

Dr. George C. Fraser
PowerNetworkingConference.com

CONTRIBUTORS

BONUS VIDEOS AND AUDIOS

The following 19 interviews found in the *Viral Networking for Drastic Results* book were excerpted from the *Drastic Results with Toni Harris Taylor* show.

To watch the full videos and listen to the full audios, visit https://bit.ly/ViralBookInterviews

INTRODUCTION

Networking. The thought of networking makes many people shudder. Many would rather take a hot poker in the eye than network. Even though I teach my clients how to network, there was a time *I hated* networking. Okay, hate might be a strong word, but I thought networking was a waste of time.

I would get dressed up, take my fancy business cards, show up to the networking event, pass out cards, return to my office, sit at my desk and wait for the phone to ring. The next week, I would show up to another event, repeat the process, and nothing happened. To say the least, networking frustrated me! That is until I met a sales and marketing coach who told me to pay her $6,000 for a 90-day course to learn how to network. Six thousand dollars! I knew I needed to learn how to get it right, so I took a drastic step and withdrew money from my retirement plan. I was desperate, and I wanted so badly to be successful. Now, I not only love networking, but I also teach my clients how to network correctly and love it!

Networking has literally changed my life. *Everything* I have in my life came from my networking efforts, introductions from my network, referrals, or direct connections. My husband was even a referral! Networking has the power to change your business and life. But only if you get it right.

My saying is, "Show up, be up, follow up to blow up!" The first challenge to networking success is to show up. Showing up in the right places with the right people who can help you grow your business. Show up also means helping other people before you get help. When networking, you can't be desperate. Networking is a lot like dating. If you show up at the party with a desperate look in your eye, no one will want to talk to you. You will be a turnoff and people will steer clear of you. It's the same way with networking. Showing up is your opportunity to plant the first seed and nurture a new connection. Our contributors share what it means to "Show Up" and how showing up took their business to the next level.

The second part of successful networking is to be up. Be up means to have great energy and to have a helping posture. Be up also means to look attractive to attract people to you; not a superficial attraction, but to have personality and energy that piques the curiosity of your connections. My brand, Drastic, piques interest and people want to know more about it. What do you have that is unique that makes you stand out? Learn from our contributors what they do to "Be Up" when networking.

The third part of networking is to follow up. This step is the one that is missed by even the most experienced networkers. The fortune is won in the follow-up and lost in the lack of follow-up. Following up is the one crucial step that, if missed, negates everything else. Having a solid plan to follow up is critical to networking success. In this book, you are going to read follow-up strategies from our contributors. These strategies have grown their businesses and changed their lives. When you use them, they will do the same for you. When you implement the *Viral Networking for Drastic Results* strategies, they help you to get known, get connected, and get paid to make six figures and beyond. Networking isn't easy, and when you don't do it right, you can waste a lot of time and money. It is my mission to help as many entrepreneurs as possible to learn how to network the right way. I'm on a mission to stop the passing of business cards and to start the building of relationships. Implement the strategies of this book and it will not only change your business, but it will change your life!

Drastically yours,

Toni Harris Taylor

ANDREA ALEXANDER: ANXIETY EXPERT & COACH

ANDREA ALEXANDER is a Life Upgrade Coach. She says, "Change your Language and Change your Life." Her background includes 15 years as an educational instructor and department director. She has over 10 years of sales in corporate America.

She left corporate America desiring to share what she had received from doing her on work in this modality—walking herself into forgiveness and recovery from childhood sexual trauma.

PHONE: 832.966.1451
WEBSITE: EmbodyCommunity.com
EMAIL: Andrea@EmbodyCoaches.com

5

I dedicate my chapter to my mother, Dianna Deane, for her ever-expanding belief in what I can do and who I am at my core. To my business partner, Carrie Muchaw, for her vigilant will and willingness to stay in love and patience with me and in all we do and build together. To my father William Brock for the way he hears me. I am eternally grateful to you all.

Today, we have Andrea Alexander, a guest author for the *Viral Networking for Drastic Results* book. She's the life upgrade coach and she'll tell you what that means in a minute. She's my life upgrade coach, wow. Look out, y'all. Where am I going to be if I get upgraded? Thank you so much, Andrea, for participating in the

book and sharing your story of how networking has given you drastic results. In your own words, who are you and what do you do?

I'm a victress. I'm a life upgrade coach. What does that mean? My business partner, Carrie Muchaw, and I, our go-to, is, "Have you ever heard everything happens for a reason?" What we find is that most people are living in the "what happened," and they hold themselves as victims. They are blaming others for their station in life, and all the things that have happened to them and have created conversations like "Oh, life is so hard and, oh my God, poor me."

Well, those experiences are here for us. We're here to get the gold out of what the experience teaches us. Are you living in the experience? Are you living in the reason for the experience? My personal path has been from victim to victress. I had childhood trauma, and when I found these tools that I use as part of my daily practice with myself and began jumping in to save my own life, I found the value in that. That has moved me to where I am today. I said, "I'm going to give back" because that's what we're here to do, share what we receive.

I have hired you to coach me. My first session was around trust. By the time this airs and is published, there's probably going to have been more sessions but, I don't love doing the inner work.

You said you hated it. Thank God, we know exactly where you are.

But I trusted you and Carrie, and I played as much as I could, full out, but I will continue to work with you all

in upgrading my life. People join me to help them, and I end up getting more out of it than they do. That's what networking is. How did this idea for your business come about? How did you and Carrie partner?

I have been in corporate America for many years and had literally educated myself into a corner. I started out as a chef and then got a master's degree. I was in education. I chose to be out of the kitchen, then sales in a similar industry seemed to segue. I enjoyed what I did for a really long time. I had been on my own personal journey for over 20 years and had covered a lot of ground and done different types of therapy. Something in me knew there was more for me. I came across a class that I went to that was completely out of my wheelhouse that seemed to say something similar to what I had been hearing. What they talked about was consciousness. I then went to a retreat without knowing what to expect. Eight women participated in "immersion," all doing the same thing to understand our feelings and our parents, and that things come from lineage and collective consciousness. We all have these same feelings, we're running the same patterns, but it shows up differently. I remembered that life is for me, and my fear of death left me in that experience. I kept going back because I was receiving so much, and I was saving my own life. This community of women, how we bonded and connected, raised up each other, leaned into the things we were most afraid of. How we supported each other in power, courage, and love was more than I could ever have imagined. It was available in friendship and love. In those rooms and in those retreats, I met Carrie. She and I had been playing and going for ourselves and doing for ourselves what nobody else could do for us, because that's what we're here to do-raise ourselves. I had come to a place with my corporate job where I was over it. I was choosing to really play in the coaching field because I was receiving so much and it was fun for me. I am obviously passionate about what I do and what I can help others create for themselves.

What I heard in that story is because you showed up at a retreat, you met Carrie, and now you are partners. You've come together, built a brand, embody community, and have decided to start networking. What made you start networking?

Carrie and I were doing all of these things. We were teaching classes; we had our retreats; we had our email campaigns, and all this stuff, and our business was growing slowly. I spoke to another woman that I know from the community, who you also know, Angela. Angela was talking about all this stuff that she was doing and how her business was growing and shifting and moving. I asked, "What are you doing?" She says, "I network." I'm like, "Oh, okay, I'm going to try that." Actually, my AC guy came out in the next couple of days, and I asked him about networking. Because he has a small business that he's grown himself, he shared a person's name with me for an NIA in another town, and Carrie and I went out there. We then met Lela Smith, and she mentioned you. I went looking for you and I found you. Then I said, "Hey, Carrie, we're going." What most people already know about Toni is that her energy calls people to come in and play. I drive across town although there's a much more convenient group near me, but I choose to play with you. What I've heard from other people is, it's not that we go in and we're trying to get business from each other within the group. We are connecting with people who know other people, all the time in all kinds of ways. For us, for them, for ourselves. I've met people that are great for me on a personal note. I've met people that are great for me on a client note. I've met people that are great for me in a business aspect. I'm building my business using the people that I'm doing business with, that I'm playing with, who are supporting me and learning how I do what I do, who connect me to others, and so on and so forth.

When it comes to networking, there are so many emotions. Some love it, some hate it. On the networking emotion meter, where do you fall, and why?

That's fun. I am an eight. I really enjoy coming to our regular meetings. People are so fun and kind, and I really love the national calls too, because I get to meet so many other people. I'm still learning to book it while you're on the call. Book it then and there for the appointment and ask for it. It's only been a couple of months that I've actively been doing this, and my feeling is I've taken amazing strides. Do we have the kinds of results where our business is expanding immediately? No, not yet. It's okay, because we are looking at sustained growth in life, and we do that with quality, not quantity.

Virtual networking. It's become more popular since the pandemic and will remain long after the pandemic has gone. What tips can you share with our audience to maximize virtual networking?

Show up. Show up. Show up! Yes. Put your lipstick on and have your mascara ready to go. The first time, the very first call, I had no idea it was going to be on camera, and they were putting us in breakout rooms. I was like; *I wasn't prepared for this,* but I stayed anyway. That's one thing that I'm great at. I just keep going back. Sometimes it's super easy and other times it's a little more distracting. What Toni has done for us is she puts so much on the table for us to enjoy, from morning coffee connections to afternoon lunches, to products that are available for us in our monthly calls and she's funneling us to other networks to find. She doesn't believe in competition. We are all evidence of what we can all do and how we can support and play with each other in multiple ways. This is what I believe networking is really supposed to be. My experience in the past, and even with some of the other stuff, is a little more self-serving. I belong to some other groups, and I frequent some other groups. They are a little different. What I know is that we got the connection queen.

You explained how you became an entrepreneur, but has it been easy? That's a laugh, right?

Yes. Because what I did is I took a massive leap of faith. I turned my 401k into a sunshine fund. I thought, in 90 days I'll be making money. But I made more money in the first 30 days than I did in the first six months. It's okay. I prepared my way for this. What I had imagined, how it would sustain me, is shifting. This is awesome because our business is expanding. Along the road, I support myself. What I'm aware of is, it's fear that keeps us from doing the things that we desire to do the most. Because of the way Carrie and I play, and we play in consciousness, we're aware of what fear is. What is failure? Failure is laying down and not getting up. Carrie and I have tried all kinds of things so far. Have we felt one thing was a failure? No.

It was this has yet to work. We're going to do something different. We can figure it out quickly, you know, two months in and we're like, okay, this isn't working, we're going to try something different. Now we have more people at our fingertips to support us in what we can do differently. We called on you. What's your suggestion? Carrie and I are experts at being coaches. We are masterful in what we do. We own the value of what we bring to the table in our coaching skills. I have a business background; I have a master's in business. But still these pieces that we are required to walk through, we require support and having someone to bounce with.

Tell me about a time that you didn't want to show up. You pushed ahead, went anyway, and I think you mentioned it when they invited you to that private retreat, and you're glad you did.

That first retreat. The very first time I went to that class, we were in that room and they were talking about the retreat itself; they were vegan and vegetarian. I thought *somebody might see me hungry*. I don't know what that's going to look like. We all have our own fears and our own limiting patterns. That's why I backed out and I started figuring out how to do it by myself. I realized I couldn't get it all by myself, that I required a coach. I called the coach. I was doing it with the coach, and she said, "You are ready for the work, Andrea." I had to think about it. I said, "Let me call you back." I had to pray about it. I had a very profound spiritual experience that moved me forward into saying yes. When I got in the car to go, my God, I think I cried almost the whole way. I was so afraid. That's just the ego, like a little self, being afraid, knowing that something's coming. It was hilarious. When all the women got there and we were all sharing, everyone had something they had been through. Then I said, I'm going to sit by the door so if I need to run, I can bolt. It was one of the most terrifying experiences I had ever taken myself on. It was the very first time I ever chose to do something completely for myself, of my own accord, to spend that kind of money doing something for my own well-being. Obviously glorious, because look at me now.

Tell me what challenges you have with networking.

The only challenge that I have really experienced thus far is remembering to ask for an appointment on the spot. When I meet somebody because I've had the experience of meeting people that I'm like, oh my God, I really want to connect with you.

I emailed them, and I never heard back. That's one of my lessons, actually create the meeting on the spot. As I said, it's only been a few months, learning where to say yes, and where to say no. Because what I'm aware of is, there's a lot of different type businesses out there and people are playing in a lot of different types of second- and third-income streams. I'm learning. Do I require that product? No, but I know some people who might.

Talk about a time when networking has made a big difference in your business. I know you just started, and it might be before NIA. I'm thinking about your showing up with your tribe. How did you meet Angela?

I met Angela at a retreat. The women that I have met at the retreat of faith and wellness through my coach and the programs and learning my tools have changed my life.

Social media is a form of networking. How has social media helped you to grow your business?

What we have found is, that social media has yet to really be massively supportive of us. That's okay. I know how it works. There are other coaches that I watch and I follow, and I have found those through social media. They have really given me a great foundation and some ways to play in my own business that are super supportive. We use Facebook groups; we use Instagram and we have a lot of followers. Because we're still a new business, we're still learning how to play with those tools so that we get our conversions. We've got great followings. Our content has been good, and our videos are great. How we've actually been able to monetize it is still something that we're playing with. Once we have more things settled, then I imagine that will change.

Okay. I can help you with that. We'll talk about how to do that. What mistakes have you seen entrepreneurs make when it comes to networking?

Not showing up. This is newer for me and I've yet to experience that. What I would imagine would be the number one mistake apart from not showing up is not asking for what you require and talking about yourself instead of asking about others. Yes, they want to hear our stories. What we're doing, we're sharing that to support people in identifying. But they want to hear about them. They also want to talk about themselves. Once we understand their needs, we can say, "I can help you with that. Let me show you how I can. Let me tell you about this and that."

In exchange, the reverse of that, a networking tip is to show up and listen more than you talk. Would you agree with that? Now you have said show up multiple times. You know that's my saying. I'm all about showing up. But I need you to define what showing up means for you.

Oh, my goodness. Showing up is being willing to be on time. Going when you don't want to. Speaking when you have very little to say. Or listening. It is being willing to say what feels uncomfortable, it's being willing to try new and different things even if you don't want to. It's choosing to choose for yourself because you have to. It's making a commitment to yourself, to your partner, and to others that you can be held accountable, that you're trustworthy. Showing up is what we do for ourselves, and it's also how we teach others how to treat us because we show up. It's a combination, the culmination of being fully committed to self and for others.

I love that. For others. Okay this is a hard one. The fortune is won and lost in follow up.

Oh, we suck at follow up. Which is why we are vigilantly playing with our follow-up programs. Because we've had gaps. This is where we've played with failure and things that have yet to work. We had VAs and there was no return on our investment. We just shifted from one into something else. Now we're playing with how to get that all up and running, because we're aware, you get to work, and we're very aware of the value that it will bring for us.

Describe how you have gone viral.

I am aware of the power of my presence. I'm tall, I'm curvy, I'm attractive, I'm vivacious, I have a lot of energy, and I always have something to say. The viral may have been positive or negative in some respects, but I'm aware that I leave an impression on people in some form or fashion. I'm aware that people are drawn to me because I have a solidity about who I am, and there's a solidity to the confidence that I carry in myself. There is a lot of peace and ease that people find in my presence. People are often enthusiastic about the things I'm enthusiastic about, and sometimes maybe I'm over the top too, just ask my mother. I imagine that in social situations where I've been in business and in work with customers and clients, when I was teaching at the Art Institute, everybody knew Chef A was the bomb; just don't make her mad at you. I was the only female chef in a group of 20 and had lots of students. They still come to me and say, "I remember you,? Do you remember what you did for me?" I say, "Yes, I do."

Beautiful. I didn't know you were a chef. We'll have to get some samples. I love the way you described yourself and you know your confidence, and I love that. We're about to close. I'd like to know what's your favorite quote around networking or connecting.

"The most important things in life are the connections we make with others." We may have no idea the kind of impression we are going to leave with someone. I feel that even more profoundly at this stage because I'm aware. What I do today, people don't always get it right away. I've had sessions where I thought, *that was terrible. I did a terrible job. They didn't even feel anything.* They came back to me and said, "Oh my gosh. I dreamed of this metamorphosis of butterflies overnight, and I saw myself... Thank you!" The women and the people we connect with show up.

I'm telling you, I create amazing miracles with the people I touch. We require connection and community to thrive in life, period.

I know. You and I are both extroverts. I mean, even I have times I don't want to deal with people. I think we all need to recharge our batteries, but it makes me sad sometimes when introverts use the excuse that they don't want to show up because they're an introvert. Don't let all those extroverts make the money.

That's just their great fear. A great fear of being fully seen standing in your light, standing in your power, and we are required to lean into that. Thank God I was born courageous.

I don't know that I was born courageous, but my circumstances certainly turned me into a courageous person. What final thoughts can you offer to those who are hesitant to network?

Get moving. There's nothing to lose. It's win-win everywhere. Even in the worst-case scenarios, you find better ways to not do things. You meet people... It's silly to reserve yourself and to stay and try to do it all by yourself. No. Find people who can support you and do it in a fun and friendly way. Other people who are doing the same thing, because that's why we have networking groups ... to support one another so I can learn from you, and you can learn from me.

STAR BOBATOON: STORYTELLER COACH

STAR BOBATOON has over 30 years of experience as a performer on stage and screen, as a litigating attorney and as a top performing trainer. She utilizes her diverse background to help speakers, coaches and business owners level up their storytelling and presentation skills, and master the art of public speaking. Star was Program Manager for Les Brown's speaker training program and ranked the #1 trainer for a national training company.

PHONE: 323.929.7827

WEBSITE: StarBobatoon.com

EMAIL: Star@StarBobatoon.com

Dedicated to my beautiful children.

Today we have another author of the Viral Networking for Drastic Results, Ms. Star Bobatoon from Fairfax, Virginia. She is a storyteller, speaker, coach, and trainer, and she is my BFF and we met networking. Star and I have been a part of a SiStars mastermind for the last eight years. I can't even believe it's been eight years. We started because we were all working for a training company that was really, for lack of a better word, pimping us. We decided to come together to build our own six-figure businesses and every single one of us moved on from that company and have created amazing opportunities for ourselves. I just love

you and I thank you for being a part of this project. In your words, who are you and what do you do?

Thank you, Toni. I am Star Bobatoon. I'm a public speaking and storytelling coach. I believe that every time you speak it is a performance and every place you speak is a stage. I empower, train, and coach, mostly professional women, to give dynamic performances on every stage they take, every time they speak.

Wonderful. Listen, she's amazing. You bring a little acting to your presentation so that it will give you more confidence and clarity, and conversions. The question is, why did you start your business? How did your business come about?

I started out as an actress on stage, on television, and in the movies, and absolutely loved what I did. But at the height of my career, there was a lot of tension going on in my family. I assumed it was because of me because I was successful, and so, in all my infinite wisdom, when I turned 18 years old, I said, that's it. I am done. I'm done being on stage. I'm done being in the spotlight. I took my gift; I took my voice, and I put it in a box, and I taped that box up and put it up on the shelf and I left it there for 25 years, trying to make other people happy by diminishing my own light. In the meantime, I had a good life. I got married; I had a couple of kids; I became an attorney, and life was good. Everything was fine. Have you ever had that feeling where nothing is wrong, but something's not right? That was the feeling that I had like I wasn't fulfilling my purpose. I'm not doing the thing that I was brought here to do. But I was not about to give up the life I had.

In the course of a year, my father died, my marriage fell apart and my job went away. Everything that defined me was gone. I just sunk into this dark, depressing state, and didn't know what to do next or where to go. Then, one of my friends invited me to a personal development seminar. Can I just say, I did not want to go. But I went anyway, and that is where I saw Les Brown.

I'm going to stop you right there because one of my questions actually goes into that. I'm going to pick up that story. This is a cliffhanger, so stay right there. You've got this business. You've pushed yourself to get out of your comfort zone. Take the proverbial box off the shelf, untape it and open it back up. What made you start networking?

As a professional speaker and trainer, I travel all around the country doing keynotes and training and people eventually ask, "Hey, can you help me?" That is how I started coaching people. But what I realized the work that I do is really about helping professional women discover, deliver, and develop their messages. What I do is help professional women become unmuted because I know what that's like. I know what it's like to mute my voice. I feel I get my greatest joy from helping other women, and men as well, amplify and illuminate their voices so that they can own their stages. In the beginning, people came to me. But it wasn't enough to sustain me. People said you got to go network. Apparently, staying at home in my house was not bringing me business.

Now it's hilarious because you all know I'm the networking queen. Literally, I must push and shove her.

When it comes to networking, there are many emotions around it. Some love it, some hate it. On the networking meter, where do you fall?

Toni, I've been in front of audiences of up to 2,500 people and I am absolutely comfortable. But put me in a room to network… I will put on a smile and do it, but I am not happy on the inside. Can I tell you why? I kept thinking I'm supposed to network to find business, to find people to work with, to sell myself. "Hi, I'm Star. This is what I do. Do you want to hire me?" I hated that. I'm doing small talk, but in the back of my mind, I'm thinking, "what can you do for me?" I was a three or a four out of 10. I think since I started actually listening to you and realized that networking's a whole different ball game, I think I might actually be up to a seven.

Virtual networking has become popular since the pandemic. You're in the national NIA group, which is a virtual group. What tips can you share to help fellow entrepreneurs maximize virtual networking?

My greatest tip is going to be to have your story together. Know your story, not just your pitch. Hi, I'm Denise and I do financial analysis. Not that. I'm talking about your story because people don't really want to know what you do, or your title. What they really want to know is who are you, and what makes you tick? The number one tip that I have for networking is to know your story and be able to tell your story in one minute, two minutes, in three minutes. Be able to tell the story that tells the world who you are, what you have, and why they should care.

You and I know the intimacies of the ups and downs of entrepreneurship. What is your driving force to stay an entrepreneur? You are qualified to go get a job and don't think we hadn't thought about it. Both of us. What is your driving force to stay an entrepreneur?

I've spent my years in corporate America, most recently working as an attorney in a law firm. While I loved the work that I did, I didn't like all rules. There was always this feeling that someone else controls me, someone else controlled my time. They tell me when I can take a vacation; they tell me when I can take off; and they tell me whom I need to work with. What I love about being an entrepreneur is the freedom. I drive what I do, and I decide whom I want to work with. I don't have to work with everybody. I get to decide the time that I put in. I still sometimes put in 70-hour weeks, but I feel like I'm doing it for me. Plus, the best part of being an attorney for me was the impact that I had on clients. I wasn't seeing a lot of that, but now when I work with people, one on one, or in a group, I get to see the transformation. I get to see when the audience goes 'ah ha' and I love that.

Absolutely. Okay. I want to pick up on the Les Brown conversation with this question. Tell me about a time that you didn't want to show up. You pushed ahead, and you're glad you did.

Well, that would absolutely be when I lost my job, my marriage went away, I lost my dad, and my son got sick. It was a time of yuck. It was just a dark place. A friend invited me to this personal development seminar. I absolutely didn't want to go. I bought the tickets when I was in a good mood, but that mood had long passed. It was in Aspen, Colorado, so I had to get a hotel. I had to get on a plane; I had to do all of that, and I just didn't want to. But I did. I'm sitting in the audience and onto the stage comes world-renowned motivational speaker Les Brown. Les is dynamic. He's telling stories. He's making me laugh. He's making me cry. Then, Toni, he starts to have a personal conversation with me. Yes, there were 2,000 people in the audience, but he had a one-on-one conversation with me. He talked about the many, many people he's impacted in his career and how grateful he was. Then he talked about his greatest regret. His greatest regret was the people he did not serve. He did not impact them because he was hiding his voice. Because he was not doing the thing that he was born to do. That was a conversation for me because I had put my voice away 25 years ago. That was it. Before that man got off the stage, I had signed up for his program. I ended up training with Les and working with Les. I traveled internationally with him and spoke on various stages with him. I ended up running his platinum speakers' training program. That changed the entire trajectory of my life. It changed my life because I showed. I showed up kicking and screaming, but I adjusted my attitude and became open to what the universe had for me. That's where I ended up.

Now you and Les are like brother and sister. He calls your son his nephew. We don't have time to go into how that evolved, but that was life-changing. It's amazing how things just flow when you show up. All right. Here's the next question. This should be a good one for you. Tell me what are the challenges you have with networking?

I don't want to. I get all this anxiety. I don't know what to say, I don't like this feeling of trying to sell myself in this one-on-one. I don't like the feeling that I'm desperate to get work. I don't like the feeling of a person doing the same thing to me. What do you do? Scan the room for someone else who's more interesting. But like I said, it's shifted, especially since I actually hired you. It's one thing when your girlfriend tells you something, but then when you pay her money, you start listening, so it's changed.

She doesn't want to when she says that she really doesn't want to, but here's what I want to say about that to everybody who's watching and reading this in the story. Even though you don't want to and you push ahead, magic happens when you're in the room.

Magic happens. But here's why the magic happens -- because I've been taught what networking really is. It's not about selling myself. It's not about passing out my cards. It's not about getting as many cards as I can and getting as many people on my email list and then barraging them with who I am and what I do. That's not what it's about. Once I learned that networking is about creating relationships and connections, it became so much easier. When I change the focus to let me be curious, what can I find out about you? Because I'm a storytelling coach, "What's your story?"

Tell me about a time when networking has made a big difference in your business.

I can't think of one time in particular, but it has definitely helped me with my business. Being in Les Brown's community made a big difference in my business and my life. I met a lot of friends there who have hired me, whom I've hired, and whom I've collaborated with. Those connections have given me opportunities that I never expected. I just closed a client recently. We met about three years ago at a networking event. Networking is like planting seeds in all of these gardens. You don't know what or when the harvest is coming. Sometimes the harvest, like a bamboo tree, takes five years to show fruit, but those things come back. As I said, it's hard for me to specify. Last year, I went to your viral networking event. I went there for love, to support my SiStar. I am listening to you break things down and I'm listening to your clients tell their success stories. Toni told me to do this, and I made X, Y, and Z. Toni told me to do this and my entire business changed. Then you gave us the challenge to set one-to-ones with people. I decided to give it a try. I end up doing about five one-to-ones, which is a simple thing. Then you actually gave us the format for the conversation. This was easy-peasy, and it's not selling at all. I loved it. I did one-to-ones with various people, and that netted me personally about $25,000 from clients and collaborations. They're not just working with me; they are working with the people that I'm connecting them to. You make it so simple, so easy, so non-threatening, and it worked.

Social media is a form of networking. How has social media helped you to grow your business?

Social media is another one of those things I'm not interested in; however, I've put videos and content on social media. I have a YouTube channel, Starpoints, short motivational messages. I've been putting them out there. How has that helped my business? The thing is, it gives me visibility. I have had keynotes through a speaker's bureau where they say they saw my name, but then they went on social media to check me out and loved my stuff. That's why they hired me. That's how it worked. It's not a direct thing, but that I'm out there, people can see me, see who I am. My personality is out there. So that has been helpful.

I really want the audience to see this. You mentioned seed planting earlier; so, meet somebody at a networking event. You do a one-to-one. That's the planting of the seed. The fertilizer is social media. As they keep seeing you, those sprouts are coming up in their mind that one day I'm going to work with her. Then one day, three years later, they give you a call. What mistakes have you seen entrepreneurs make when it comes to networking?

When it comes to networking, "Bob, can I have your card? Here's my card." "Here's my card. What do you do?" "What do you do?" It's just cards, there is no relationship. That's one of the biggest mistakes. I think that one of the other big mistakes entrepreneurs make when it comes to networking is not having a plan. What is your plan? What are you doing? Why are you here? Then the next biggest problem is not following up. I've had a potential client say, "Oh ,my God, I definitely want to work with you. Send me a contract." I did not follow up, and the opportunity vanished. Follow-up is the biggest thing that people need to do. My tip is to have a purpose because that will allow me to get in the room and not pass out and follow up.

What does it mean to you to show up?

It means to be intentional. Take the time to figure out what it is that you want, what it is that you're trying to accomplish. When you know that you show up differently, you show up like a boss; you show up confident; you show up self-assured. So that is what it means to show up, just to be clear on those things. Also, because I'm a performer, showing up means owning your space, and physically owning the space you're in. Your body language speaks volumes before you even open your mouth. That's what it means to show up, and the results are phenomenal.

What's your best strategy for following up?

Toni told me to do this. When I'm at a networking meeting, pull out my phone and set up the one-to-one right there. Oh my God, please don't give me your card. If you give me your card, it sits on my desk, and I don't do anything with it. But the best thing for following up is setting the one-on-one at the moment. When I go to NIA meetings, go to networking, and set it then. That's the best way to get that done.

Describe how your networking has gone viral. Let me clarify this question because when people hear the word viral, they think it's millions of views and likes on social media. But viral can also mean what people are saying when you're not in the room. What has the one connection sprouted off?

It's interesting. The way I know it's gone viral is how many people talk to me and they already know me. I did a speaking engagement where I shared the stage with former first lady, Michelle Obama! I'm asking myself, "how did I get here?" I was talking to the president of that company that hired me. I had to ask. There are some great people in this room. Why did you choose me?" She starts talking about my reputation. We spoke to this person and that person, and that person recommended you and this other person knows you. I was like, oh, that's the networking gone viral.

What is your favorite quote about networking or connecting?

My favorite quote is from you. "Show up, be up, follow up, to blow up." That has to be it.

That came to me and it has stuck like glue and guess what? To everybody that's watching and listening and reading the book, you can create your own quote.

Absolutely. I believe that every time you speak, it's a performance and every place you speak is a stage. That would be the start of my quote.

What final thoughts can you offer to entrepreneurs who are hesitant to network?

Join a group and get a coach. The "by yourself thing" is terrifying, and it takes so much longer. When I join a group and come regularly, I'm no longer the stranger and it makes me feel better. When I have a coach who talks me down when I'm feeling crazy, I do better. I would just say, don't do it alone. Join a group, get a coach. Those would be my final words.

DIANNE BOWDARY: FINANCIAL LITERACY COACH

DIANNE BOWDARY is a corporate executive, career coach, author, motivational speaker, and financial literacy coach. Dianne is a master at leveling up the human resources in others to achieve their greatest potential. Dianne is the founder of the Stay Hungry Club, an organization that provides education and tools necessary for women who want to do more, be more, and give more in their personal and professional lives.

PHONE: 833.269.3279

WEBSITE: DianneBowdary.com

EMAIL: Dianne@DianneBowdary.com

To the brave women hungry to take on everything life has to offer and have to step out of their comfort zone with networking. Become a blessing to others and be blessed by the fruit of your labor.

This is the interview for Ms. Dianne Bowdary for the *Viral Networking for Drastic Results* book. Welcome Dianne and thank you for the opportunity to interview you. Have you ever authored a book before?

I have co-authored two books. The last book is *Beyond 2020: Life and Business Lessons on Thriving Amidst a Pandemic.* Dr. Lynn Richardson, my business partner, and friend compiled the book with 14 amazing contributing authors and MC Lyte wrote the foreword. I'm excited about the lives that continue to transform through the lessons.

Whether you're a collaborative partner or writing it from scratch, it is a big feat to get a book done. I'm glad you're a part of this group. Would you tell us who you are and what you do?

I am a corporate executive, and I own multiple businesses as an entrepreneur. A term I frequently use to describe myself is a corpreneur, which encompasses both roles. I am most excited about the Stay Hungry Club®, designed for ambitious women who are also corpreneurs ready to take on the world yet, crave to take their professional and financial lives to the next level.

What made you come up with the Stay Hungry Club®?

There was a time when I was working in corporate and thought I was on my A-game. I was on a career track with a company where I thought I'd work through retirement. I was buying whatever I wanted, when I wanted it and lived a dreamy lifestyle. The fateful day came when I no longer had that job; I realized I'd taken my role and pay for granted. I was stuck looking for a new position that matched my salary requirements. After six months of looking, I'd lost my drive, hunger, and appetite for life. Even though I achieved multiple promotions and received many awards for my previous work, I started questioning my abilities. That self-doubting attitude spilled into how I handled my money; therefore, spending plentiful was reckless. You would think that after the experience, I would have learned my lesson.

The reality is I had several cycles of having lots of money and then having none. I finally came to a point when I was at the bottom, where I realized I had to make a change. I started taking finance classes and implemented what I learned. I followed strategies to live my life as a business to make money consistently and put my money to work for me through multiple investments. I was sad and angry about how my life had turned out, and I realized I couldn't be the only one running on the hamster wheel. I actively sought financial coaching training and made a tremendous transformation in my life and my legacy. There was a compelling force to share the knowledge with everyone. I wanted to provide the tools and resources in a safe space where like-minded women would join together to encourage and celebrate the successes of working toward financial independence. Through the roller-coaster experience and ending up on top, I learned the importance of staying hungry for what life has to offer, going after what you want, and never giving up despite the circumstances. In addition, it's much easier to keep going when you surround yourself with like-minded people. The struggle is real, but you don't have to go through it alone. Hence we have the birth of the Stay Hungry Club®.

I love that you are helping people with that. Networking is the theme of the book. You and I met networking in 2014. What made you start networking? Was it somebody's advice?

I received sage advice from encouragers at Between Job Ministries to help with my job search. It's funny what you'll do when the need arises. The encouragers told me,

"You're not going to find a job sitting behind a computer; nobody knows that you're just filling these applications out online. It can feel like your resume is falling into a black hole. You've got to get out and meet people, even when you're not in the mood."

It was a job search, and talking to corpreneurs. People think putting their resume on a job site is the way to find a job. But I know from personal experience that it's all about who you know and who knows you. Did networking help you find the job you needed?

Absolutely. Networking contributed to all the subsequent job offers and promotions. Often, networking must happen first, and then the right people will learn about your abilities and experience. There's no question about it; I would meet someone who knew somebody who knew someone else who was instrumental in my job search. Coupled with my reputation, work ethic, and performance, I would land the interview I wanted. I could not have done it without networking.

When it comes to networking, there are many emotions. Some love it; some hate it. You rarely find people that are in the middle. Where do you fall on the emotion meter when it comes to networking?

When I first started, I hated it. I thought it was superficial small talk. I don't like being phony and felt I couldn't be myself. Networking had negative connotations that I processed going into my first event. Nobody's going to want to help. I need to mingle within my industry and not people who don't care about a stranger. All these harmful thoughts ran through my mind. But then I discovered soon that I could change my mindset about networking. I now started to shift from how networking couldn't help me to how I could help someone else. Now my emotion meter reflects a love for networking, and I make it a point to create the time whenever possible.

Virtual networking, because of the pandemic, has become popular, and I know we are doing this virtually. What tips do you share with entrepreneurs to maximize virtual networking?

There are two tips I'll share. When you get into a video conference, you may hear, "Put your contact information in the chat." Then you're trying to pay attention to what people are saying while furiously typing out all your information with the links. I've heard people say, "Oh, I forgot to add my email, or I just noticed a typo." My first tip is to have all the information typed out so you can copy and paste it into the chat. You don't have to worry about typos or missing data; you can focus on the speakers. After seeing the impact firsthand, I share it with everyone I encounter. The second tip is to give the other networkers an easy way to contact you. Another trick I learned from you was to create a URL, such as https://meetwithdiannebowdary.com/ and connect it to a calendar link. I've found that when I use my meeting link in the chat of a networking meeting, I will have a few meeting requests for one-to-ones or business consultations in my inbox. That's never happened before.

Exactly. In the past, we would go to business events. In virtual events, the travesty is coming to the event and leaving with the chat. When you put your link in, people will click your link. Every time I leave a virtual link there, I am determined to get three to five appointments and I get them. Now you're corporate, and you have a passion for corporate. You already told your story, but entrepreneurship is hard. You could easily stay on the job. What's your driving force for being an entrepreneur?

It's not so much a focus on being an entrepreneur and working for myself. I feel a sense of urgency when I start my day. People in our families, communities, and the world are one check or one crisis away from loss of income, poverty, homelessness, and hopelessness. They could have $500 in the bank or $500,000. Will they keep their money, or are they up to their eyeballs in debt? Is the lifestyle sustainable with their income? Are all their eggs for income streams in one basket? God put the mission on my heart to help people create their recipe for financial freedom. How can I connect with more people to change the mindset, behaviors, and outcomes of their financial independence? How can I further help my clients to become owners instead of consumers, to get the trust of their families, and protect everything they worked so hard to build? How can I help my clients to get out of this rat race of losing a job, not having any money, getting a job, having money, and getting it all eaten up by taxes with nothing to fall back on? How can I get my clients off that playbook? I've seen many people have professional and financial breakthroughs, which fuels what I do as an entrepreneur.

You must have a passion for others. Your why can't be about you. Your why has to be about the people you serve. When you help people, and your why shines through, you'll be able to put your kids through college or retire, whatever your goals are. Your why needs to be about helping other people. Tell me about a time, when you didn't want to show up, pushed ahead, and were glad you did.

There are many examples of that, especially when I first started networking. A time that stands out is when I was severely down about my job situation and had been looking for a while. I had shown up to a few of the networking events, and while they were helpful, I felt like I had to put on a face to attend them. Sometimes I was in the wrong space in my head.

I spoke to a mentor, and he said, "You know what? You're just being selfish right now."

I replied, "I don't know what you mean."

He repeated, "You're being selfish. You're only thinking about what you can get out of this. Some people will show up, and they need you. They're waiting for you."

I was confused, "That's impossible. They don't even know me."

And he replied, "Well, they need what you bring, and no one else can bring it but you. If you don't show up, they can't experience that and appreciate it."

I felt guilty on the one hand, and on the other hand, I was curious. Who would need me for whatever I offer, especially when I felt so broken? As you've said, Toni, it's not about me. It's about how you can help people. I ended up going to one particular event. It's not like the event was intended for folks who didn't have a job; it was a networking event for business owners in the community. I ended up going out of curiosity and guilt. While there, I introduced at least three people who needed connections and were appreciative. In hindsight, it was hardly any work to get them connected. In addition, I ended up meeting with folks who helped get me interviews for positions that weren't published anywhere; The employers were looking for internal referrals. So that experience changed my mindset. Networking only works if you and others show up in authentic form with an open and serving approach.

That was a textbook-perfect response because if we push ahead, especially when we don't feel like it, we have no idea what's in store for us. I can tell you story after story when I did not want to show up. I'm the networking queen, but sometimes I don't want to show up either. Then, "Oh, my God, I met this amazing person." That was beautiful and golden. Because we're experienced networkers, we make it seem effortless. But tell me, what are some challenges you have with networking?

Part of the challenge is the follow-up. It's easy to forget or neglect; you're all engaged in talking to folks and getting all this information during the event, which is excellent. Then you leave, and you return to other priorities. It may be your business, your nine-to-five, or whatever happens at home. It's easy to get sucked up in that. You may intend to follow up in the next day or two. Next thing you know, a week, a month, a quarter, and six months have already passed. Then, it's next year.

Is it too late? It's never too late to follow up, but there is something. You make an excellent point. The biggest challenge of networking is the follow-up. And I think the strategies you shared earlier that I teach of getting people on your calendar when you're in front of them eliminates the need to follow up.

Absolutely. You stress the importance of making things systematic; that applies to business, and we use that in our nine-to-five. We make processes as automated and organized as possible to eliminate the chance of errors or not happening. Having the link there automates the process of following up because now you've got this invite on your calendar, and it's going to pop up. If you live by your calendar, you're either going to attend or reschedule the one-to-one. Still, you'll have a time commitment there, which is a tremendous help when you want to be intentional.

You've already shared that networking has helped you get positions, but I want you to think about how networking changed your life or the moment you went "wow."

I attended a networking event with several business owners. They were very much like me in that they had a lot of dreams and aspirations they were actively working on. My coaching and consulting business was in place, and I was trying to put all the loose pieces together. I learned from that networking session that there was a significant need for something like a Stay Hungry Club®. People wanted a safe place where no one would judge them because of their level of ambition or their high aspirations. It was confirmation for me to launch The Stay Hungry Club. I wasn't going to think about it anymore. They gave me the confirmation that I needed to push forward. Had I not participated and met all the extraordinary talent and resources, I wouldn't have been as connected to the needs and wants of other corpreneurs. Instead, I got the final stamp on my decision to launch the Stay Hungry Club®.

I love that. We know social media is a form of networking. How has social media helped you grow your business?

I will tell you that I'm not there yet with social media. I understand the importance of it and the influence around it, so I am getting to work with the tools. Now I've been using it for about two years. Still, I'm just now starting to get in, especially with Stay Hungry Club®, to leverage the power of influence and connecting with people through social media. I love making it very personal and interactive, unlike before. My new challenge for myself in 2022 is connecting to folks more personally through social media. I'm looking forward to it.

If you're intentional and drastic about asking to connect with them on social media, that's the way people get to see you, and it validates who you said you were. It makes it clear you didn't forget me; you and I lost touch for a long time. I believe you didn't fail me because you kept seeing me on social media. And when the time was

right we connected. Social media is an extension of your contact. What mistakes have you seen entrepreneurs make when networking besides not following up?

I would say going into these events for the wrong reasons and not being genuine or not fully present. They'll approach you, make small talk and not be interested in what you have to say. They're not asking the questions to learn more about you. Instead, they show up and throw up about their business. People will pick up on that immediately if they are not fully present or genuine. The people who could be your ideal contacts are less likely to schedule one-to-ones, or they won't respond to your attempts for follow-up.

On that note, what does it mean to you to show up?

Showing up is being present. We go in with a plan. What's my purpose for going to this networking meeting today? I want to come out of here with five connections. Instead of what I'm going to get out of it, what will I give? That's my best networking tip. That, and be true to yourself. That's what showing up looks like.

Show up with the position of giving versus receiving. This book is about viral networking. Describe how your networking has gone viral.

My networking has gone viral thanks to NIA and your coaching. It's not limited to the people local to Texas, where I reside. I now connect with people with unique skills, talent, and intellect from the country and worldwide. As an example, one of the national NIA calls had representation from Canada, Alaska, and Panama. I did not have the reach I have today. Viral networking has taken my business to a new platform for offering services and collaborations. These new relationships have been game-changing for me personally and for my companies.

I know you said not following up was a mistake many people make. Do you have a good tip for following up with people?

In addition to putting your link for scheduling in the chat, schedule the one-to-ones before you leave the event. If you can't do that, when you get back to the office or at the end of the day, do not lay your head down until you have made an appointment with x number of people from the event. Either get their link, send an email, or call them. Set a realistic goal and stick to it. Schedule the interaction. For instance, I put in my calendar, every Wednesday and Friday evening at a particular time, I will reach out to at least five people, most of whom come from a networking event. That way, I'm sure to follow up with folks. If you make that a habit, put it in the schedule and on the calendar, and then stick to it, follow-up becomes a habit and second nature after a while.

You are absolutely right. What is your favorite quote about networking or connecting?

My favorite quote for networking must be from Zig Ziglar; there are a lot of good quotes out there, but I think this one is my favorite, "You can have everything in life that you want if you just help other people get what they want." It's inevitable. It comes right back around to you. To do this selflessly and authentically is the only way to go.

JEANNA BUMPAS: INSURANCE ADVISOR, HEALTH & WELLNESS COACH

JEANNA BUMPAS is a God loving woman, wife, mom, daughter, grandma, sister, and friend who has overcome many obstacles and attributes her success to gratitude and seeing the positive in all situations. Since July 2012, she has created a growing community of like-minded women who strive to be the best version of themselves in all areas—physically, financially, spiritually, mentally, and emotionally. Not only is she is a mompreuneur but she is also a multipreneur, who helps families and businesses protect their assets with all lines of insurance in the state of Texas.

PHONE: 832.527.8402

WEBSITE: JeannaBumpas.com

EMAIL: JBumpas@Alumni.Rice.Edu

I dedicate this to all the moms out there who have ever doubted themselves. Thank you for allowing me to be a part of your journey! You are stronger than you think and the best is yet to come!

Today you all, we have one of my best friends and I know you all say, "Toni, you just love everybody," but Jeanna is super special. As you hear our stories together, you'll see why. Jeanna is the most resilient woman I know. She's probably a bigger, drastic stepper

than I am. She just doesn't call it that. But she has been through so many challenges, from being a caregiver to her parents to being totally flooded out in Harvey. But I've got to introduce you to my good friend, Mrs. Jeanna Bumpas.

Thank you, Toni. Thank you for that amazing introduction. Yes, I love our friendship and it's just grown so much more than just business and networking. So very blessed to have you in my life.

In your words, Jeanna, who are you, and what do you do?

Well, my name is Jeanna Bumpas. I am a wife, a mom of four, a grandma to six babies, three bonus babies, and a caregiver. My passion is to inspire and motivate Mompreneurs to be the best that they can be. To show up for themselves, because when they can show up for themselves, they can show up for everyone else in their life.

She's also a Network In Action member and in Network In Action, she's a multipreneur, like most of us entrepreneurs. In Network In Action, tell us what business you represent?

In Network In Action, I represent insurance for both personal lines and commercial lines insurance in the state of Texas. Then, of course, because we network, we can always help people outside of the state of Texas as well. But that's what I do here in our amazing NIA group.

I want to stay focused on the Mompreneur Business, because it is such a heart-centered, passionate business, and frankly, insurance isn't sexy. If you want some insurance, talk to Jeanna.

You are correct, insurance is not sexy until you must use it, and when you're cashing that check, it's pretty sexy.

Let's talk about that for a minute. Did your insurance business come out of your personal experience of being flooded? Was that part of your inspiration to go there?

It absolutely was. Several years ago, I decided I needed another stream of income. We need multiple streams of income and because at one point Toni, when I had all four of my children at home, our auto insurance bill was over $1,000 a month! That was like 10-12 years ago. From the consumer side, I knew what I needed and wanted. Then once we got flooded after Harvey, I was a big advocate of flood insurance for others. I knew if I could help a family save money, get them equal or better coverage with more discounts, it's game on. Then I learned the commercial side of it, because doing all the networking that we do, and we're going to talk about networking here, I meet a lot of business owners. I wanted to help business owners with errors and omissions, professional liability, general liability, and all that good stuff. I am multifaceted on both the commercial side and the personal side, but that's exactly how I got involved with it, because of my personal experience.

It's amazing how many people in the book have taken their personal negative experience and turned it into a positive one for their business. I think that's how your health and wellness business started as well. Give me the background on your health and wellness business.

At one point, I was almost obese. I worked in corporate America 60 plus hours a week, traveling an hour and a half to and from work both ways, so three hours on the road, and 12 plus hours in a chair at a desk. My health just got out of control and during my corporate wellness exams, I'll never forget that one day, they're like, "You are one pound away from being obese." I'm like, "What in the world?" I truly believe timing is everything. A couple of weeks later, I was introduced to an amazing program & supplements along with some amazing people that are still in my life today. I took my health into my own hands and made it a business as well because let's face it when you do something that you love and you get success and you're pretty good at it and you can invest, invest in yourself, learn it and teach it to others; and that's what you do, Toni, right? Invest in yourself, learn it, teach it to others, then it just makes things easy and fun. I learned how to take control of my health, get my energy back, lose some weight, and be the best version of myself so I could help everybody else that I'm always used to helping, wearing all those hats, and started teaching other people about their health and wellness. I've taught other people how to earn some income by doing that and it's just been amazing ever since, although, we've had our ups and downs.

We're going to cross those bridges in a minute. But think back to when you first started your health and wellness business. What made you start networking?

Well, what made me start networking in my health and wellness business was that it was a Plan B and I had a full-time job. When I was laid off from corporate America, I was thankful I had Plan B. I always tell people, to make sure they have some sort of Plan B, and keep their options open. At that point, I decided, "This is now going to be my Plan A, and I need to learn what to do. I need to grow my exposure." The truth of the matter is, I've always kind of been a social butterfly. I've always volunteered in the community, so that was a form of networking, but it was for the community. It was never to grow a personal brand or a personal business, or so I thought. I was just used to being out there.

Then I became involved in some local organizations, and began building relationships, but the real key in any networking is not what can I get, but what can I give? When I'm able to add more value than what I receive, blessings are going to come. Right? I really think getting out there, meeting new people, and building those relationships is vital. Toni, just like us, we have known each other eight or nine years now, met at an event, and didn't conduct business immediately, but we made an impact and added value. Well, you added more value to me that day than I added to you, and I kept your number. When the time was right, we reconnected. You never know whom you're going to meet. I always say, just be a good human, because you never know when your paths are going to cross again.

When it comes to networking, there are many emotions. People either love it or they hate it. On the networking meter, where do you fall when it comes to networking?

It's interesting that you say that because during COVID my networking meter got low. I wasn't into networking because I got used to being lazy and staying in my leggings every day, my hair in a ponytail, and no makeup. I didn't want to meet people, even on Zoom, because I just didn't look presentable. That's where just having your self-confidence in the way you look and the way you feel is important. But honestly, on my networking meter, on a scale of one to 10, I'm an 11 because I love to be out there networking. When I had to be behind my desk, it is torture.

Yes, you do love networking and connecting. Speaking of the pandemic, virtual networking has become more popular. Even though you don't love virtual, I know that you made it work and expanded your business. What tip would you give someone who's doing virtual networking?

It has expanded my business. The tip is to show up. Show up, be presentable, and for me, I must get dressed up, fix my hair, put my makeup on, but also put on some music and just kind of find my groove and jam. I feed on energy from other people being in an environment. Here, in my home or office, I personally don't have that energy and those people to stimulate me. I'm putting on some music. I'm dancing and jumping around before we hop on any virtual networking meetings.

In 2019, the rug was pulled from under your business. After all of that soul searching and figuring out what to do next, what's the key driving force that kept you as an entrepreneur? Because it isn't easy.

It's not easy. It's honestly easier just to go work for somebody and be told what to do, show up and leave.

Entrepreneurship is not easy. But really, that driving force is knowing that I have a voice that needs to be heard, that makes an impact in women's lives, that makes this world a better place. That is why I show up as an entrepreneur helping Mompreneurs.

Sometimes we overthink it, but I love the simplicity of that response. Tell me about a time you didn't want to show up, you pushed ahead and you're glad you did.

There's many different times that I didn't want to show up, whether it was in personal relationships, family events, business, things of that nature. First, let me just say, I'm thankful Toni, for the NIA experience. I know you introduced it to me about a year prior to me saying yes. I believe everything happens at the right time. For the right reason, I'm glad I showed up when I did. But taking it back, I'm glad that I showed up and continued my entrepreneurship because when that rug does get ripped from underneath from you, there's many doubts that set in. Can I do this again? Do I have the energy? Do I have the stamina? Do I have the strength? Do I have the know-how? Do I have the knowledge? Do I have the products? Do I have everything? Will people believe me again? Will people trust me again? Will people follow me again? I'm not going to lie, like I really thought about not showing back up into this world of entrepreneurship. But I'll tell you why I'm glad that I did, that I pressed forward, got on that boat, raised my flag, and just went. It's because of the impact that I have made on other women's lives.

It was not easy. The other thing, when it's not easy, we have to remember it's not about us. Pushing forward is for the people you haven't met yet. We all have challenges with networking. Even though I love networking, I have my challenges. What challenges do you have with networking?

Oh my God, Toni, my challenge with networking, is following up. The F word.

It is. If I have interviewed 20 people, 19 have said that. It's a consistent challenge. Following up. But it's the key to success with networking as well. So, hold that thought because another question is going to come in that line. Tell me about a time when networking has made a big difference in your business.

I believe, and I'm trying to compartmentalize, like I've got the insurance side, which really helps, but I've got my other side, which I love to focus on, my health and wellness and my coaching and mentoring. Here's where it's made a huge difference. Just showing up, being visible, in person, on social media. I have a rock star person on my team right now; she is amazing. I talk to her every day. I love her. We really connect. Honestly, she was in the insurance industry as well, so we connect in some other areas. But on my health and wellness team, my coaching team where we help Mompreneurs be the best that they can be, she said, "You know, I've been introduced to this concept by other people and I've been approached by other people to do what you're doing Jeanna, but I saw you out there. I met you at the networking event. I saw you on social media and

I knew you were the person I wanted to lock arms with." Because of that, Toni, I told you the other day, I had my biggest month last month. She is part of the reason we had that biggest month, but had she not seen me and met me at meetings and seen me on social media, that probably wouldn't have happened.

Well, I think you probably pre-studied these questions, which by the way, she had not seen, because the next question is, social media is a form of networking. How has social media changed your business?

It has changed my business. I'm going to give you all a secret sauce tip for social media, and everybody has what works for them and what doesn't, and things like that. But I'll tell you one of the things that has worked for me, for my brand, for my social media, is to be that person of inspiration, of encouragement, of motivation. There are so many bad things that go on in the world. I don't even watch the news. You turn it on, there's just horror story after horror story. There's so much negativity out in the world and people need a breath of fresh air. They need to have life poured back into them. For me, I choose to keep my social media uplifting, and positive. I'm not going to talk about politics. I'm not going to talk about controversial issues. Not that I'm against any of that, because you know my belief, but I'm just going to keep it positive and that's just me. That is what I believe has helped my social media grow, my following grow, and I'm always having to delete friends to add friends just because of having that positive, encouraging presence out on social media.

You do it best. I emulate you. You have a great community, so continue to do that because you are amazing.

I do want to back up because something just came to my mind. I had a high-level leader in one of my prior companies and then actually another leader in my prior company of which I had no relations either come to me and say, "I'm very impressed about how you handled that whole transition. Someone from the outside would've never known what went on and all the details, whereas we weren't seeing that elsewhere." That was just affirmation and confirmation of what I'm doing on my social media is working.

Yes, I agree, you are amazing. What mistakes have you seen entrepreneurs make when it comes to networking and what's your best networking tip?

There are several mistakes I see entrepreneurs make. They go to a meeting and they're handing out their business cards and they've got commission breath. That doesn't work. Get rid of the commission breath because it truly is when you connect with other people and you ask them, "How can I help you?" Toni, I learned that from you. What do you need today? How can I help you? That's the number one tip. I will say when it comes to follow up, ask how can I help somebody? I am not lacking in that follow-up. You tell me what you need, I'm helping you. The follow-up I'm lacking is in my own personal business follow-up because it's more fun helping other people grow their business than it is to help yourself.

When you help others, you are helping yourself. It all comes back full circle. So, what's your best strategy for following up after a networking event?

The best strategy for following up after a networking event is number one, set an appointment during that networking event. Get it on the calendar so that you have a reminder and make sure calendars are synced. So if you're using a calendar on your phone and a team's calendar, whatever method you use, make sure that they are synced. But then the other thing is, I truly believe one of the things that help me, helped me be successful in corporate America, and I've transitioned it over into my entrepreneurship. That is at the end of the day, download everything from your brain, from your phone, from your computer, whatever it is on a pad, on a piece of paper. Write it down, whatever journal type you're using and get that out of your brain and onto that piece of paper, so you can truly relax in the evening time and go to bed with your mind clear. That way you can wake up ready to kick butt the next day. But yeah, whatever calendar system that is, make sure you're using it and set that appointment immediately.

Describe for me, Jeanna, how your networking has gone viral.

That's a great question. Obviously doing virtual Zoom meetings and things have gone viral. You and I actually took a trip to Canada several years back and I've made relationships, met people, and made friends. Since that time we've stayed in touch. Then with social media, there are no boundaries. There are no boundaries as far as where you can take your business on social media and so it's been pretty amazing that way.

One connection begets the next, begets the next, and so on and so forth. We're almost down to the wire. What's your favorite quote about networking or connecting?

"The Best is Yet to Come." I've had that for a long time, probably since the early 2000s, and it's your mindset. It really comes down to, don't settle for anything less. There's always going to be better. Don't accept the status quo. Whatever you did today, you can do it better tomorrow.

What final thoughts can you offer to entrepreneurs who are hesitant to network?

I think the most important thing is to find you a networking buddy. When you do things alone, number one, it's a little intimidating, and it's not as fun. Find you a networking buddy, you'll talk ahead of time. Toni, whom do you want to meet? Jeanna, whom do you want to meet? Then it's always easier when you're out networking in person, for me to go find this person whom you're wanting to meet, "By the way James, you need to know my friend, Toni," and make that introduction. I like to network that way, but let's face it, there's going to be times when you're networking with people, whether you're virtual or in person, and you're just like, that isn't my cup of tea and I need to get out of this conversation quickly. Right? There's nothing wrong with that. You can be upfront and honest, "Toni, I loved meeting with you. I've got to run. I've got an appointment." That's something to consider because your time is so valuable. Just make sure you honor your time.

MARVIN D. CLOUD: BOOK PUBLISHING CONSULTANT

Marvin D. Cloud founded mybestseller Publishing in 2004. Since that time he has helped thousands of authors across the country to successfully navigate the independent publishing landscape. Marvin is embarking on a journey to help business owners, entrepreneurs, thought leaders, and visionaries, to write and publish message books whose ideas will change the world.

PHONE: 832.881.0402

WEBSITE: MybestsellerPublishing.com

EMAIL: MarvinDCloud@gmail.com

I dedicate this chapter to my grandson, Marvin D. Cloud II. You are destined for greatness.

Today my guest is one of my *favoritest* people in the whole wide world, Mr. Marvin D. Cloud; whom I met in 2012. We have collaborated and published several books together. I'll let him tell you who he is and what he does, but I'm going to tell you this man is near and dear to my heart. Welcome Marvin, how are you today?

I am doing well. I'm so excited about this opportunity to be interviewed by you once again.

To be a part of the *Viral Networking for Drastic Results* book. Marvin, in your words, tell everybody who you are and what you do.

Well, my name is Marvin D. Cloud and yes, that D is important to me. I am a book-putter-together person. I do everything someone needs; editing, layout, cover design, ghostwriting, whatever someone needs to get a book put together and put it out on the market. I can help with that.

I love what you said to me recently. You said "Toni, there was a time I would do any book project," but now you're focused on books that serve the world. You called them message books. Tell us more about that.

Yes. Not to contradict you, I wouldn't do any book, but almost any book. But now I'm more concerned about the direction the world is headed, or it's already in. I want to be a part of positive change-making, change-bringing, impactful books. That's all I want to do. I think that is my calling now. That's what I'm looking for: people who have a message that they want to get out, that they want to share with the world. That's what I'm doing.

I love that. That's what you should be doing because you're a positive person. You're positive energy. Any departure from that is not operating in your natural space. Well, how did you become a book expert, a book putter togetherer, because I know you've had several iterations in your life.

Yes, it really started out as a fluke. I had another publishing company where I was publishing a magazine. When I had my magazine, people would come to me and ask me about publishing books. But I didn't know anything at all about it. But one day a guy who many people in Houston know,

Robert McKinley Gilmore, had this book that he wanted to do called *Hope After Dope*. It was the book about his story of being on crack and other drugs and things like that and then recovering to where he was now an adjunct professor at Texas Southern University. Again, I didn't know anything about the book publishing industry, but I helped him put this book together and he went on to sell a bunch of copies. I thought to myself, *Man, this could be a good business.* But at the time, the holdup for most people was that printers wanted you to print 3,000 copies. Even at $2 a copy that was still $6,000 that you had to pay for inventory. But then a couple of years later, they came out with a new technology that allowed you to print 50 copies or even one copy, and it made it affordable. That's when I started seriously looking into book publishing, and I started in 2004.

Any idea how many books you've published?

Well, I can tell you the average is 100 titles a year. That's the average, 100 a year. Now some of those may also be reorders or something, but according to my printer, that's what I'm responsible for, on average, 100 titles a year. So, over an 18-year period, we'll be looking at close to 1,800.

Well, I love that. So, let's talk about networking and how networking has helped your business. What made you start networking?

You. I was networking, but I was doing it kind of haphazardly. I think most people, when they start out, they just think, "Hey, I'm going to go pass out business cards, collect business cards, see what happens," with no game plan or no strategy or anything to it. When I say strategy, not only talking about how I can get business, but how I can help somebody else. I did networking because I knew it was important, but I just didn't really know how to go about it. But things drastically changed for me when you became a NIA franchisee. It has just really opened things up to me. To be honest with you, I know I am not using NIA to 100% capacity, for various reasons, but it has nothing to do with the organization. Of course, most people know I've been ill for the last couple of years. However, I've seen enough of it to know its value and to know that it works.

Absolutely. When it comes to networking, there's a meter. People either love it or they hate it. My question to you is where do you fall on the meter and why?

You know, so this is it, and this is being really transparent. I love it when I do it. When I think about it, sometimes it can be overbearing, or something that I just said, "Well, I don't have to do this, or I don't feel like doing this today." But every time I show up, something happens that impacts my bottom line. You know? For the most part, I love it. I love meeting people. I love talking with people. I love being around positive people who are trying to do some things I'm trying to do; who are positive about their own business and things like that. I'm the only entrepreneur in my immediate family, so there are some things I can share with my siblings, but they're not going to really get it. When I can talk to one of the members who have gone through something, who understands exactly what I'm talking about, whether it is a marketing question or a tax question. It helps you because it's not all about just getting business, but it's about making connections and making connections for life.

Connections for life. I know, when I'm long gone, that some of those connections, will be still playing together. But you also said a very important thing. Networking brings community. It brings together like-minded people because entrepreneurship can be very lonely. Especially if you're a home-based entrepreneur. It can be extremely lonely. If you don't have those people that you can commiserate with when things are hard, celebrate with when things are great, then a lot of people go out of business because they are lonely. Networking is popular is because it brings community.

I think that's why sometimes we, as entrepreneurs, think about taking a job. It has nothing to do with our business model, or whether we're profitable or not. But sometimes it's just you want to be around people.

You want to be around people. I tell people all the time they join NIA for referrals, but it really becomes family. Let me just say for some of my members, I'm the mama. It really is like children. But I love it because they still love each other. It comes with a fondness for one another. We're talking about NIA, which is in-person networking, but since the pandemic, virtual networking has become very popular and will not be going anywhere soon. What strategies or tips can you share to maximize virtual networking?

Well, the key to networking for me, whether it is in person or online, is in follow-up. There's no point in getting a connection if you will not follow up. Now that doesn't mean that you're going to do business with each other next week. You may not even do business ever. I get so many referrals from my networking group. People call me all the time and say, "Hey, I got your number from such-and-such." That's just how things have really grown for me. But being in a pandemic, which coincided with my recent illness, which had absolutely nothing to do with COVID, I was laid up for over a year and am still in recovery. But I do a lot of networking online. I do a lot of meetings, a lot of one-to-ones, a lot of group meetings. But networking online is as valuable, or more valuable, than networking in person, because you can do that at a moment's notice. You can do an instant meeting with somebody. Now, I get a lot of, I don't really call this networking, although it is, people call me for information, then they say, "Well, do you mind if we get on a quick Zoom meeting?" Or something like that and say, "Yeah." Because people want to see. This is kind of like the Jetsons' era. Now we can see people, and it helps with that comfort level, breaking down when someone is a stranger or something. They can see you too, see that you are a real person and all of that.

Absolutely. So, you've already talked about how you came into entrepreneurship, but listen, any of us could get a job at any time. What is your driving force for staying an entrepreneur?

There are a lot of reasons. Some of them are selfish. One is that I used to work for Dow Jones, Inc. It published the *Wall Street Journal*. I went there when I was 18. The idea was to work for six months. I went there; I was 18, and I left at the age of 28. I realized that what I was afraid of was about to happen. I was going to be in a corporation for 30 years, get a gold watch, which I don't think anybody does that anymore, but get a gold watch and a pat on the back. I never wanted that. I've always felt driven to do something, and that's not a knock against people who work at jobs for long periods of time, not at all. But for me, I wanted something that I could control, where I could call the shots, where I could implement my ideas of business. Actually, I told the church about my first entrepreneur business, and I know you don't know this, but I owned a hog pen. I sold pigs with my uncle, my mother's youngest brother. That was my introduction to being an entrepreneur. We bought and bred pigs and raised them. Then we sold them at auction. That was a different business, of course. But I said that to say this, you can be successful at anything you want to be. Everything doesn't have to be a suit and tie and all of that. That went well for a while until our interests changed. But I've always just had that bug to do something different. Now I have the opportunity to do something different that could be big.

Wonderful. Tell me about a time that you didn't want to show up, you did, you pushed through, and you're glad you did.

Oh, wow. That's probably been numerous times, which serve as a reminder, because sometimes when I really don't want to do something, I just think about what happened last time. I go there, because what I found for me when I put the emphasis on making money, or the potential money that I can make, it never goes well. But when I put the emphasis on serving people, the money follows. Sometimes there are just times when your body is tired, or you are mentally drained, and you must push through. Then when you go there and you're like, "Man, this was one of the best times I've ever had." You're meeting people and you are sharing things with them that can help them. It turns out to be better than you thought.

Tell me about your challenges with networking.

I do the bulk of my production myself. There was a time when, of course, when I was a lot younger, when I could do a lot of the technical stuff overnight. The only thing I want to do overnight now is sleep. During the daytime, there may be some networking opportunities that I have to pass up, simply because I have to get jobs out. It is not really the challenge with networking. It's the challenges with how I'm operating. One thing that I'm trying to do within the next year is to get more assistance, to turn over some things because I've been on a computer for 40 years. The eyes are not what they used to be. The hands are not what they used to be. The energy level is not what it used to be. I used to could operate on four to six hours of sleep. I can't do that anymore. I don't kid myself about that. There are some things that I would like to train other people to do, or partner with other people who are already doing some things that I'm doing so that I can do what my real love is in the publishing field and that's teaching people how to write, how to get those stories out of you. My big dream is to go around the country doing workshops and seminars. I don't know how long COVID is going to be with us. I know that has slowed down that part of the dream, but I can still do workshops and seminars online.

Tell me about a time networking has made a big difference in your business.

This may sound self-serving to me, and even to the NIA group, but the truth is just truth. Last year in November, when I was a sponsor of your conference; and one thing that people must understand the relationship that you and I have is almost like, if you say, "Marvin, go jump off this bridge. But I guarantee you it's going to be worth it." Then I take you at your word because you have never said anything to steer me in the wrong direction. When the opportunity came for me to be a sponsor at your conference last year, and as you know, I'm right out of my sickbed, I don't have the funds to do it, but I knew if I did it would work out. We worked out the financial arrangements. Thank you for doing that, because I told you I don't have it, but if you would work with me, I'll pull it out some type of way, because I knew it would come. Man, that was one of the best conferences I've ever been to. The business more than paid for the sponsorship fee.

Joining a group specifically to give and receive referrals, that's a strategy. But if you're just waiting for somebody to send you a word-of-mouth referral, listen, that is a gift. There is nobody who must tell anybody about who you are and what you do. Consider them as gifts. But you can't build a business on that. I see too many small business owners sitting back, waiting for somebody else to tell somebody about them. It's dangerous. It's too sporadic. It's all over the place. You've got to be very strategic. My next question is about social media. Social media is a form of networking. How has social media networking helped your business?

It definitely has helped, but I have to be honest again, I'm not doing it anywhere near the level that I need to be doing it. Most of my social media is simply Facebook. I get some things from LinkedIn and things like that, but I know you get out what you put in. If you don't strategically set up a social media strategy, you won't get anything. Then what you should do, and I don't want people throwing things at me and all of this, but you can't be an entrepreneur and always want to talk about where you ate. Give people something that's going to help them do better, be better, or something like that, in order to get them to follow you. People post about their cats and dogs and all of that. That's fine for what they may try to do. But if you are a business owner, you need to find more strategic ways, because it's not about likes, it's about sales. You can get a million likes and not make anything. You can get 20 likes and get 20 sales. If that's one of my weaknesses, it is social media, but I'm addressing all of those things because when you've been laid up for a couple of years, you get a lot of time to think and review and know what you need to do and know what you're going to do differently.

What mistakes have you seen entrepreneurs make when networking and what's your best networking tip?

First of all, I'm a people person and I know a lot of entrepreneurs, aren't. However, when you go to an event, and you just sit there and don't participate, or don't introduce yourself when opportunities arise, then you're kind of squandering that networking opportunity. I think a lot of people come to an event without a plan in place. The plan could be something as simple as "I'm going to meet four people." Instead of saying, "Hey, there's 60 people here. I'm going to grab 60 business cards," which you can do. But if you say, "I'm going to talk to four people," really talk to them, and find out what their needs are. What do they do and how can you help them? You're not necessarily going there saying, "Hey, I'm Marvin Cloud, book publisher. I can help you, blah, blah, blah. I can do a book for you or whatever." To me, you're kind of like selling yourself, which we all are constantly selling ourselves, I get that. But when you go and take a different angle of "How can I help you?" It may not even have anything to do with what you do. But I do know that when you sow those types of seeds, they come back. So that would be one of the things, just going to a networking group without any expectations, that is kind of backward.

My saying is show up, be up, follow up, to blow up. When I say show up, what does that mean for you?

That means you must participate with whatever it is. There are no organizations that don't expect you to show up. If you are a student going to school, they expect you to show up, in order for you to get the lesson. If you are a member of a church or whatever, they expect you to show up. If you are part of a business group, you never know what opportunities that you can run across just by showing up. When I spoke the other week, with the 10-minute spotlight, I walked away with three or four potential clients, because they liked what I was talking about.

You mentioned earlier not following up is a mistake that a lot of entrepreneurs make. What's your best tip and strategy for following up?

Now, it can be automated. At the worse, you can have a reminder, and that's not if you're not going to go fully automated, but at least, a reminder to check your logbook or whatever. But now there are different CRMs and things like that available to help you manage your leads. They can send out emails, text messages, and even let you know it's time to make a phone call. You must have some type of system in place if your concern is to scale. If you're not that concerned, it depends on what you want to do with your business. But you need to have some type of system in place to help you manage your leads and your follow-up.

I love that. Of all the interviews I've done, you're the first one to talk about automation and systems. All right, so describe how Marvin's networking has gone viral since working with me.

I get calls, and inquiries from all over the country. Different people who have seen me, or heard from me, or sometimes you invite me to other events that are nationwide. Just by, showing up and being there, people see you and they call or they email you and they want more information. Those are things that, either you're going to have to spend money or spend time. If you have a lot of money, then you can do all this advertising and things like that. But if you don't have an advertising budget, then you show up at networking opportunities. I've been invited to speak at certain events simply because I've networked with you. Your reputation is such that sometimes I'm so used to having to send a lot of stuff to different people to prove who I am. But when people call me and say, "Toni Harris Taylor said to call you," and I say, "Okay, well, what do you need me to send you?" "Nothing, really. Just want to know if you are interested." I'm like, "Yeah, I'm interested." That's just how it works. It goes back to what I said at the beginning. You have never steered me wrong. From doing your small, first starting off type of events to where you are now, you just never steered me wrong.

SHEILA COLLINS: THE RESET REALTOR & VIDEO MARKETING COACH

Sheila covers the Houston real estate market. Her fast forward out of the box thinking, motivated attitude, and genuine care for all her clients has awarded her a rank of Top Producing Realtor®. She spent the first 25 years of employment in the general construction industry, where her innate entrepreneurial spirit, went unanswered. After a leap of faith, Sheila "reset her life" by becoming a realtor in her 40s.

PHONE: 713.289.4908

EMAIL: Sheila.Collins13@gmail.com

I dedicate my chapter to my dad.

Today's guest for the viral networking conversation is Mrs. Sheila Collins, The Reset Realtor, as well as the video coach who helps you succeed with video. I just said who you are, but in your own words, who are you and what do you do?

First, I am a mother of two sons and a grandmother of two grandsons. When it comes to my career, my bread and butter is being a realtor. Through video, I tap into my creativity and have merged it into my style of doing business. It's something I have found I enjoy doing.

Let's start with the video side of the business. I know I kind of shoved you a little into making that a business, because you were good at it. You were great at attracting

your clients with video. But you have a story that explains why it is really drastic for you to do video.

I was a little girl who did not want to be seen, but in life, you cannot hide. I was born with a birth defect called Crouzon's Syndrome, which is a facial deformity that affects your eyes, ears, nose, and throat. I looked different from the way I look now because I've had multiple surgeries throughout my childhood. Some were lifesaving, and some were because they were needed to give me a better quality of life. When I was 12 years old, I had major reconstructive surgery, and that was life changing. I was blessed enough to live in a city where we could afford surgery in the medical center, as well as the specialist doctors.

As I grew older, I had some other major medical problems that had nothing to do with my birth defect. With each surgery, I thought I would get better. I hoped it would give me a better quality of life and no one would make fun of me. Much later in life, while at the 2020 Reset Conference, I realized I have spent my life going through resets. I realized that when people are buying real estate or they're selling real estate or they are leasing real estate, or even doing commercial real estate, it's a reset.

I am proud of you because honestly; you struggled with accepting that brand. But the way you describe it now, you have embraced it. It's perfect. You got it. You are the queen of resets.

I own my style of business. I came from the corporate world, where we lived in a box. I was told what to do every day. It was not until I became an entrepreneur, a real estate agent, that I had to figure things out. No one is telling me every day what I need to do. If I want to be successful, I need to figure this out.

What made you start networking to grow your business?

I was looking to grow, so I started networking and quickly realized that I enjoy it. If you want to be successful, you need to know how to network. You need to know where to network. You need to surround yourself with the right networking people. Honestly, it was not until I joined NIA and met you; I learned how to do it. Well, here's the other thing I remember when I first became a realtor, I knew nothing about real estate. Honestly, I didn't even know a realtor. I knew I wanted to make it. I got into the business, and I learned as I went. But when I hit my three-year mark, I thought, *this is pretty good.* Every year I was getting better, but I also wanted to improve, therefore I hired a business coach. We started working together, and I was floundering, and paying a lot of money. I lost a contract, and I was getting fearful. What happens when you get fearful? You get angry. On one of my calls, I started panicking. How am I going to pay this coach? I thought, the coach was the answer, but no, you have to work at it, and you have to be coachable. As I got into it, I was upset and she told me; you need to door knock, which I did not want to hear.

It was in May. It was on the weekend, a Friday, to be exact. My husband had gone out of town. I had no one with me. When things happen to me, I've learned that I tend to isolate myself, that's my personality. That weekend I stayed home and I cried. "Oh, what am I going to do?" I was anxious. This lady wants me to door knock. Finally, I literally talked to myself. *Sheila, why don't you want to door knock?* I came up with three quick reasons. One was, people are mean to door knockers, and all my life, even as a child, they picked on me on. I was made fun of. I've gone through that. I'm an adult. I do not have to do that anymore. The second reason was I'm afraid of dogs, which is ironic since I have a dog. Then the third one was, it was May, and it was hot in Houston, and I wasn't going to door knock. I had created these videos on my own as well. I started watching YouTube and started seeing these other realtor throughout the country being successful using videos. I started making these little videos here and there. But my coach told me about four years ago, "Stop doing videos, that's a waste of time."

That week I made a video and posted it on Facebook. My husband came home, and I told him how upset I was. He said, "I don't want you to door knock, anyway." That's probably the only time I listened to my husband. "My husband said he doesn't want me to door knock," I said. I was honest with my coach. However, I made myself a goal. I told myself I would create one 30-second video giving one real estate tip and I would post it once a week. The goal was for six months. I did not tell the coach this, but I did it. By August, my business started growing. By December, I had my first lead from Instagram. Whatever you pick to grow your business, focus on that. For me, it's a video.

Sheila, when it comes to networking, there are so many emotions. Some love it, some hate it. Where do you fall on the networking emotion meter?

I probably fall in the middle. I'm a people person and I'm a social butterfly. Once I get to my events, I love it.

You do it well. You do a great job of showing up. We'll talk about that more later. But you had to learn to love it. I remember when we first met you were like, "Hmmm,

this networking thing... ."

I was networking and some of the networking groups are only people who are kind of getting together. They don't really know how to network, and whom you network with is important. I made acquaintances in some groups, but many groups were more like social clubs instead of business incubators.

Virtual networking has become popular since the pandemic and I don't think it's going away. What tips do you have to maximize virtual networking?

When all the Zooms and all that first came about, I remember liking it, and I thought *this is great.* I mean, why weren't we doing this before? But again, I'm a social butterfly and I like to get out. Then, I got to where I wasn't feeling it and I wasn't excited about it. However, virtual networking is here to stay and, like anything else, embrace it if you want to be a part of something and sometimes that's all you have. For some groups, that's all you have. Not only that, but you can also expand your network. You can go to virtual events with people from different countries. You have to embrace it and like it. You must get used to that and learn how to work it. I think you're good at teaching us how to use virtual tools like copying the chat. They've given you all the tools to use. I still would rather do it in person, but I'm not opposed to Zoom.

Is entrepreneurship easy for you?

It is now. Again, I came from the corporate world for 25+ years. But I like all new things. I had to learn to be disciplined and time-focused. I had to learn to work on my own. I went to an office where I sat, and I could talk to whomever I wanted. I'm no longer in that.

The question I have then is what is the driving force for you staying an entrepreneur? Because you are social. Why do you stay an entrepreneur?

Because I have always had an entrepreneurial spirit, but I have two children who also have a birth defect, the same birth effect I had along with a couple of other medical issues. I basically had to work for insurance. But I always had that entrepreneurial spirit in me because I always wanted to be my own boss. I always did little stuff, looking back on it, I sold Mary Kay, and I sold jewelry. I would dabble in a lot of little things because I was kind of finding my way, but I could never quit my job. I wasn't bold enough. I had to be safe because I had my baby. I even took an entrepreneur class at HCC. I had to find that safety net. Then I found someone to marry me. I got married and once I got married and had that security and my kids were grown; I was ready to take that risk. Why I took real estate, I don't know. Real estate was one of those things. I said, "I'm going to take a real estate class." I got my license and left my job cold turkey and started in January 2014.

You are a drastic stepper. I know you didn't really have a framework for who you are, but now that you and I are in the same world, I've seen you take drastic steps. Congratulations. The next question I have is on that same line. Tell me about a time you didn't want to show up, you pushed ahead, and you're glad you did.

There's a lot of times I didn't want to show up to a lot of little things. Once I get to wherever it is, I know usually, I'm always thankful. This past week, we had an award show for my brokerage. I was given an award because I made so much income. I did not want to show up, although that's a great accomplishment. Out of the 1200 agents, less than 200 were qualified and considered top producers. I was one of them and I did not want to show up. I did not want to go. Of course, I knew I needed to go because it was part of the accomplishment. I needed to show up for myself to celebrate. That's something I do not know how to do. I think you know this because you're my business coach. I downplay a lot of stuff.

What challenges do you have when it comes to networking?

My challenge is not talking to enough people. Even though I say I'm a social butterfly and I'm not afraid to approach people. That is really surprising considering, you know, as a little girl I hid behind my mom's dress, and I had six older siblings who were overprotective. It was easy for me to skirt under one of them. However, in networking events sometimes I get that *oh my gosh, I got to talk,* feeling. I still have that in me, and I know I can do it. I know I can make conversation, but making that first step to talking is an awkward feeling. Being in between two people who are talking, and you don't want to interrupt. But you want to meet these people too. Or, you say, "Hey, I want to talk to this person," and you want to, but they're in a conversation. Now, that awkwardness is going around. That's my challenge, and it probably always will be. We learn to manage them better. I will hang out and meet whom I need to meet. I still get nervous about that. I've been to a lot of networking events.

Tell me about a time that networking made a big

difference in your business.

Networking made a big difference in my business when I met you. When I became a part of NIA. When I became a part of NIA, I met people who had the same mindset, and that's where I needed to be. I needed to be around like-minded business entrepreneurs. I needed to be around a good, networking queen. Any organization you're in, if you have that good top leader, someone who is in charge and who can help people and guide them to where they need to be. In NIA, that's what you do for us.

I'm actually going to answer this question for you, too. Yes, NIA has been a big piece, but I believe what made a big difference is when we went to the Reset Conference in Dallas.

Yes, that conference made a big difference because I had my "aha" moment there and that "aha" moment was "reset." Every speaker who spoke from the platform talked about what happened in their life that got them to the pivot. That's why it was called the reset conference. That's when in my mind, I thought, that's what I've been doing all my life. That's it. I've been telling myself, the surgery was okay. I know I'm going to go through this, but it's going to make me better. I know I'm going to have a recovery, and I told my kids, and I told my grandson, you're going to go through this, but once you go through it, it's going to be better. Just relax, you know, we're here. It sounds so easy, but it's hard to relax in your pain and discomfort, but you know you're there to get better. That's what nurses and doctors are for. I had a lot of life resets; my children's biological father took his own life, and I had to help them through that. My father passed away. Our family is going through a reset because of the dynamics of helping mom. They were married for sixty-eight years. I mean, it's not only medical life that resets, but we all have some type of something that goes on. I choose to look at them as resets because the resets are good. I would say, take the good and leave the bad every day. When you wake up, be grateful. Even when life is good, things happen. Everyone's going through something.

It's how you show up when life is happening. That really is the testament. Here's your favorite topic. Social media is a form of networking. How has social media helped your business to grow?

Well, I think social media has grown my business because that's all I really use. I don't cold call. I will never pay for leads. I will not door knock. I think social media is here to stay. There's going to be changes in social media. What are people doing? I think people are probably more on social media than they watch TV. I'm going to bring it up -- the slap on the Oscars. When that happened, what did people do? They grabbed their phone and Googled. *Did I just see that happen?* Social media is a fantastic tool. Social media can be like networking. You have to learn to use it. Do it the right way. I see a lot of people doing it the wrong way, but you know what? I also see them trying. The one thing I've learned since the pandemic is that for people, perfection is out of style. It shows who you are. If you see my videos, a lot of them, I just get on and I'm more on the rift kind of talk. You know, you'll hear me stutter and it's because I'm not using a script. I probably should be, but I'm not. You see me. What you see is me.

What mistakes have you seen entrepreneurs make when it comes to networking and what tip would you give them?

Mistakes would be not networking enough, picking the wrong networking groups, and the wrong network. I believe we all need to know whom to network with. I know I don't want to network with other realtors, but I want to network with businesses and get to know those people so they can remember me as a realtor. It works both ways. I can remember them as whatever trade or whatever they're doing in their business. This is probably number one, not following up, and we all are guilty of it. I know we all are. We're all guilty of it at one time or another.

We are. We're not perfect at it, but we know we need to follow up. Follow-up is your tip, right?

Network with the right people and do your follow-up. Don't be afraid to get out there. You know, one thing, and it just came to my mind, we're all probably going to that network, those networking groups with the same feeling of nervousness. If we remember that, it will probably make our whole networking life easier. Even after the follow-up, a lot of people say, "Well, they didn't follow up with me." Well, did you follow up with them?

Here's another question. What does it mean to show up?

It means to show up as yourself and to be genuine. It means showing up for other people and showing up to know that you're there to help yourself as well. Let's be real. We're all there to help ourselves. But show up and know there's someone in that room you may be able to help. If you don't show up, how are you going to help your community, grow yourself, or help someone else grow?

Showing up is not about you. It's for the people you're meant to help and serve and meet. That is excellent. You just mentioned that not following up is a mistake that entrepreneurs make. What's your best strategy for following up?

I like to use your strategy, which is to make the date right there at the event and put it on my calendar. That's still a struggle for me because I'm a paper person, and often I'm sitting there looking for my paper. But I have become better. It's a process and I've become better with my calendar and putting everything in there and deleting and taking things out. I still catch myself looking in my calendar and then going to my office and looking at my paper calendar to make sure everything's jiving. My advice would be to anyone networking, don't leave there without making a date at that event.

Can you describe how your networking has helped you to go viral?

I want to say people remember me and my vibrant personality. I'm going to tell you something, people remember my looks. That's a good thing. I actually now welcome that. People remember the way I look, and most people think I'm memorable, especially when I'm being myself. I cut up and I say silly things and I like to talk to people, just randomly. Like my son says, "You talk to people, mom. I wish I could do that." You talk to them and make small talk. I think people remember that and it makes them feel good. They remember me. I've been going to my dentist and one day I was on the phone looking at houses and she said, "Oh, you're looking to buy a house." I said, "No, I'm a realtor. I started going to her, and she said, "I might look for a house soon." I put her on my CRM and I started sending cards to her in the office. Well, she called me last week. She wants to start the whole buying process, but she told me one thing. She said she has a lot of realtor for patients, but my personality and the way I came in and showed up, she told herself, *that's who I want to work with.*

Okay. This has been a great conversation, Sheila. What's your favorite quote about networking or connecting?

It would be a quote by Brené Brown, whom I love and who has probably helped me get out of my box. "Courage starts with showing up and letting yourself be seen."

What are your final thoughts for entrepreneurs who are hesitant to network?

You need to get out of your own way. The only way you can be successful is by meeting people. That one connection you make may push you over the top. It may give you what you need, give you what you want, and attract what you need. Whatever we put out there, we attract it to ourselves. If you want to be successful, get out there and network with other successful entrepreneurs. Even if it's someone who's starting out, you may be that person who is able to help them get started and get over yourself.

DR. VANESSA DE DANZINE: LEGACY WEALTH BUILDER

DR. VANESSA DE DANZINE, is a retired NYPD Detective encompassed with more than two decades of educational consultancy. She is co-host of "Keeping it Real with Shannon," a speaker, mentor, author, journalist, community advocate, insurance producer, and financial literacy consultant/coach, a collective symphony coupled to her vast array of leadership skills to help underserved communities build wealth.

PHONE: 833.44.LEGACY

WEBSITE: LegacyInsurancePlanners.co

EMAIL: Vanessa@LegacyInsurancePlanners.co

I dedicate this to all the unforeseen families who will embark on the journey of financial freedom towards building generational wealth, thus leaving a legacy.

Today, we have another episode talking about viral networking for drastic results. My guest is Dr. Vanessa de Danzine from New York and Panama. She is half-time, so today she sits in Panama, which makes us international. Welcome, Dr. Vanessa. You are one of the coaching clients who came through the viral networking conference. In your own words, tell us who you are, and what do you do?

I'm a retired detective with the New York City Police Department. I'm an author, a speaker, and a weekly cohost on "Keeping It Real with Shannon." I'm an associate editor for a journal, an entrepreneur, a community advocate, real estate agent and a researcher. My passion is financial literacy and legacy wealth building. I'm also an insurance producer, let me not forget that.

Please don't forget that, because that's really the foundation of what you do. You are very passionate about legacy building and generational wealth building. Why is that such a passion for you?

Legacy wealth building became a passion for me during COVID where I focused on what's going on with wealth, particularly in our black and brown communities. I received a text message from a friend/coworker of mine during COVID who invited me to support her as a financial consultant with her affiliate link. She was on a platform that focused on financial literacy. While I supported her in that platform, I began to understand, yes, financial literacy is something that is lacking particularly in our black and brown communities. However, this was a platform I needed to be a part of. Although I'm aware of the wealth gap, I did not put things into the context of how it affects communities at large. However, I knew I needed to be a pillar in the community to change the narrative about money. There are too many of our people living in generational debt and are only focused on thriving to survive and not striving to get to the next level. That became my passion, to bring that message to the community and the importance of building generational wealth. I understand the fears when you think outside the box, and look at the things around you. The surrounding systems are working how they are designed to work. When you think about resources, the availability of resources, the accessibility of resources, the sustainability of resources, and a lack thereof, it's this driving force that engages me to bring community to the table with the knowledge to leave a legacy.

During our coaching, one of the big, "Yes, that's it" moments, was your market dominating position is to help regular people live their life like a business. I get excited every time I say that. What do regular people not know about living their life like a business? Just give us a couple of things, because there's a plethora.

People don't know going to work every day or going on trips or going to dinner, that they could start living life like a business. This is how the wealthy leverage their money. This is how the wealthy continue to build generational wealth and leave a legacy for their family. I travel a lot. I'm an international traveler. But now I don't travel for pleasure using my money. When I did medical missions abroad, I used my money. My traveling was considered vacations. Now I travel for business. Anything I do now is all business, and that's how I live my life. That's one of the strategies I want to bring to the table to show people. Listen, you can have fun and do things, but you must learn how to get that money back. It's really learning the rules of the game and then playing the game by their rules.

What made you start networking? I mean, you are a retired police officer and I know you must network within the system to get things done, but what about networking outside and for your own business?

I got invited to your event, the Viral Networking Conference. I wanted to learn and understand what it was. I began to understand and look at the benefits of networking. You're around a plethora of people doing great things, not just locally, but nationally and sometimes even globally. Everybody always has a product or service they can offer. I realized your event was a referral system. I could see the transparency within the network of how you can grow your business. You learn a lot of things. It was not just a referral system, but you learn how people run their business, learn what makes their business move and what makes their business grow. This is one benefit I've learned by joining your NIA networking group and I'm really learning that this is the way to grow your business.

You started networking by coming to the Viral Networking Conference and it's changing the game for you.

Absolutely. This is definitely a game-changer for me. Everybody thinks about running a business, but how do you run a business? How do you start the business? Where do you start? How do you make the business grow? What are the marketing techniques and strategies? What do you do? Social media, all these things became a new framework for me to appreciate. I just said, "Wow, I could do this. I could move this." I didn't think about a signature talk and how to engage others. It is a new phenomenon for me, but it's a good journey and I'm looking to grow my business in this capacity of networking.

Now, when it comes to networking, there are many emotions. People either love it or hate it. Where are you on the emotional networking meter?

I would say I'm about a five since I'm still learning. There is a plethora of knowledge in this space that is so rewarding. I've learned to grasp the benefits and appreciate all the meat and potatoes that come with networking and I'm excited. I guess my emotion would be excitement, eagerness, and hunger for more. It's a hustle to get it done, but I know I can get it done.

What's interesting, and I want to say this to the audience, is someone I met in 2013 invited you. I met her nine years ago. She did not do business with me until now and she brought you to the table. Sometimes with networking, it's not instant. But, when it happens, look at how it has flourished. Dianne brought you to the table. You are here now; you are expanding your business. Sometimes we must be patient with the process. I've never met you in person. Virtual networking has become popular since the pandemic. What tips can you share to maximize virtual networking?

I understand the pandemic left many people destitute, lost, angry, and scared, and they were home and out of work. This was something new for everyone and people had to go into survival mode. Like we always say, "You got to do something before something do you." People need to get involved. They need to engage themselves in networking locally, even nationally and globally, to see how their businesses can grow. There were a lot of entrepreneurs made during the pandemic. That was a good thing because people began to think out of the box and understand how they could monetarize their passion, their talent, what they normally do every day, whether it's baking, nails, hair, or tutoring. Networking is a way to expand and grow a business.

You're retired, you have many talents. You've got real estate. I admire what you've already shared with me

about your financial portfolio. Congratulations, ma'am, you live what you teach. That is amazing. But being an entrepreneur is not easy, especially and I happen to know, you've had a lot of life happening. It's like you signed up and life said "bam." What is your key driving force to staying an entrepreneur since really for you, it's not financial as much. What's your key driving force?

There are a lot of things I do where I don't get a monetary benefit or return on it and that's okay because my efforts are also to help and serve others. Being a pillar in my community, I look at the challenges. I see the struggles, the disparities, the barriers, the challenges, and the lack of resources there and people need help. For me, it's not always about making the dollar, but making a difference in someone else's life. Although I can't save the world, if I can make a difference in one or two people's lives, that's all that matters to me.

You know what? When you approach your passion with that attitude, the money comes. Tell me about a time you didn't want to show up, you pushed ahead and you're glad you did.

We know that there are life challenges. We're born, we live, and we die. We are exposed to so many things and many things can change our paths. But you want to do the best and be the best at what you do. I didn't know that the time, money, and energy required to teach others about generational debt, wealth gap, finance, and building wealth would cost me. However, I knew it was something I had to do and sacrifice. Not showing up your best could be detrimental to your business. You don't want to compromise and jeopardize the efforts you have already made to start the business. You want to be able to keep it going. That's important. These are not just ideas, I have researched finance for years. I bring over 20 years of educational consultancy, and I have partnered with Dr. Lynn Richardson on a parallel platform as a W.E.A.L.T.H Ambassador. As a vetted leader I have served as director of Community Based Organization Partners-BK, past chair, Community Based Public Health Caucus, an affiliate of the American Public Health Association, and past president, National Community Based Organization Network. These positions paved the pathway to bridge intersections of community and finance towards financial freedom. The main goal is to bring discipline, commitment, and mindset to financial freedom. Financial ruins and the lack of, perpetuates one's ability to gain wealth and to create generational wealth. Your untapped inner fears will promote you to learn how to spend less money, get more money and foremost get your money back. It all begins with changing the mindset about money. Do you want to create generational wealth? Do you want to leave a legacy? Maybe you want to launch a business. Maybe you want to turn a hobby into something more. Or maybe you have a creative project to share with the world. Whatever it is, changing your mindset about money is the first challenge that makes all the difference.

Now, I know you push ahead when things are not... Because, as I said, it's been a challenge, one challenge after another. Sometimes that happens. But the win is in showing up, right? Because when we show up, especially when life is happening, it's like the world opens to you and at that moment, you can tune out what's going on and focus on your mission. I commend you for pushing

ahead, Vanessa. You've done an excellent job. What are some of the challenges you have with networking?

Since I'm still new to networking and understanding all the things that go with it, one of the challenges I was having was creating my story. Creating that timeline for the story. Having a signature talk and identifying who my target audience is and should be, because everyone may need my service and product, but everyone is not your client. It's a challenge to talk about life insurance, death, and wealth. It's not a conversation at the dinner table every day. But it's really to bring people to the table and have conversations like this so they can stop using GoFundMe as a life insurance policy. Those are my challenges for people to really appreciate what's needed and to change the narrative they have about money.

Tell me about a time that networking made a big difference in your business.

For one thing, I have understood in a short time the power of networking. It gives me broader access to different audiences and how I can grow my business within.

Social media is a form of networking. How has social media helped you to grow your business?

Through networking, and particularly through your Viral Networking Conference, I've had the opportunity to reach out to others who had a VA connection. With this connection, now I'm able to manage my social media portfolios, connect to groups and focus on a direct target audience. It's a work in progress, but we're getting there.

What I love is that my community supports each other. When you see there's someone in the network you can

use, you are using them, and your social media is growing, it is a work in progress. But guess what? It always gives. I've been using social media for 12 years and it's still a work in progress. Keep plugging at it. What mistakes have you seen entrepreneurs make when it comes to networking?

I see that they're not being prepared. Not knowing how to market their product or service and not knowing the benefits of networking. They're just not in the know.

Get yourself in the know. Hire a coach. I remember when I first started networking; I hated it too because I was passing out cards, and waiting for the phone to ring, and that was not happening. Once I learned the strategies to network that it wasn't about selling, that it was about connecting, and that I needed to get people on my calendar immediately, it changed the game. I know you're practicing scheduling the appointment right away. It takes courage, and it's drastic to do it, but I believe that you're coming along. I appreciate that you are willing to be drastic and do whatever I ask you to do. That's all a coach can ask for. All right, in your mind, what does it mean to show up?

It means to be ready, so you don't have to get ready. When you go places, you want to be prepared because you don't know who or what connections you're going to make. You're not sure. You know that your business can go to the next level, but who will see something in your business? Who will recognize you? Who will want to use your product or service? You've just got to be prepared to just take that leap of faith and keep it moving. You don't want to turn down a connection and you don't want to be disappointed when someone confronts you pertaining to your product or service, and you're not prepared to respond or defend what you have to offer.

I love it. What's your best strategy so far for following up?

I would say be persistent. Be intentional about what you do. Hone and own what you can provide and stay connected.

You are in the infancy stages, but can you describe how your networking has gone a little viral?

Like I shared earlier since having a virtual assistant I've seen my social media grow. There are more connections, more people are viewing and liking my page. I have more followers and new friends in my network. I'm just getting in tune to really get out there to let people know who I am and what I offer. When we went over the analytics, I could see how much traffic had visited my page and people are really interested and looking into my service.

What's your favorite quote about networking and connecting?

As it relates to my passion for building generational wealth and insurance, I would say my favorite quote is, "If you pay now, then you can play later. But, if you play now, you will pay later."

That is excellent. What final thoughts would you offer entrepreneurs who are hesitant to network?

You don't know what you don't know. In order to get in the know, you must be engaged. Engage yourself. Get involved. I know it's a struggle. It's a challenge. People are not really accustomed to being outside their skin, but you must jump in that lion's den and get in there. Just go for it. Take a leap of faith.

BEA EMANUEL-SIMS: ENTREPRENEUR, REAL ESTATE INVESTOR

BEA EMANUEL-SIMS is the founder, recipe developer, and head baker of Sweet Granny Bea's, a dessert shop focused on classic southern traditional delicacies that will take you back to your childhood with every bite! What began as a hobby is now a budding small business with hundreds of customers nationwide. Bea is a serial entrepreneur as she also co-owns a real estate company. But her passion is to motivate and encourage others to take up the entrepreneurship mantel.

PHONE: 314.749.0383

WEBSITE: SweetGrannyBeas.com

EMAIL: SweetGrannyBeas@gmail.com

Dedicated to my tribe and specifically, my husband and family. Thank you and I love you. Without you, none of this is possible.

Today we're going to talk about viral networking with my client who is part of my Drastic Results coaching group and NIA member, Mrs. Bea Emanuel-Sims of Sweet Granny Bea's. Let's talk networking. But before we go there, we want to know, who are you and what do you do?

I'm Bea Emanuel-Sims. I am the owner of Sweet Granny Bea's. We provide delicious Southern classic traditional desserts. We focus on hard-to-find desserts, like sweet potato and buttermilk pie, peach cobbler, bread pudding and desserts that will make you want to slap your mama. We don't do cakes, cupcakes, and cookies, because everybody does that. We focus on those traditionally hard-to-find Southern classic desserts.

Let me just tell you, her desserts are phenomenal. That buttermilk pie, that's the one I have to get next. I'm excited about you taking me back to my grandmother's kitchen. The best buttermilk pie was my grandmother's recipe, and I haven't had it like that since she passed away. One thing that we know that makes you different is really taking that nostalgic feeling of going back to your grandmother's kitchen. The other thing you're about is food, family, and fun. Talk about that and how we've lost that art.

A new area for Sweet Granny Bea's is Soul Food Sundays and yes, it's all about family, food, fellowship, and fun. It's a video series and my goal is to bring the family unit back into the kitchen. When I grew up, my grandmother's house was the go-to spot on Sundays. We had Sunday dinner and would reconnect, love on each other, and fellowship, and it was all about the food, and the family and we had a good time. I think that this type of connection is missing now. We've become so isolated, because everybody's on their devices or on the games, or they're inundated with information, that we don't take a break and connect with live people. I think the best way to do that is through great food, connecting with the family, loving on each other, and fellowshipping.

You are right. Everybody's eating out now. Bringing Soul Food Sundays back, I love that. Let's get a little backstory of how your business came about.

In 2007, my grandmother passed away. She raised me and my fondest memory as a kid, was when she would make sweet potato pies. She didn't make them often, but when she did, it was like the second coming of Jesus. We could smell it all the way outside, and it was like, "Oh my God, she's making sweet potato pies!" All of us kids, me, and my cousins would run to the kitchen to get a piece of pie. Watching us devour the pies would bring my grandmother much pride and joy. In 2007, when she passed, a big part of me felt a void. I felt like a piece of my heart was taken, and I needed to find a way to fill that void. I began to make sweet potato pies.

In 2017, we began selling our products throughout the year. The first year we made about $35,000, the next year we doubled, and the next year we were on our way to tripling. That's when COVID hit, and we had to pivot. Last year, we had our best year yet, and the sky's the limit. We've got a lot of new things coming for 2022, and I'm really excited about our future.

I am really excited to be on the journey with you as well. In October 2021, you took a drastic step and left your full-time job. Tell us about that thought process.

Sweet Granny Bea's has been full steam ahead since 2017. We doubled, then tripled our sales. It required more and more time. Throughout this journey, I had a full-time job, and earlier that year, it was getting to where I was only working on Sweet Granny Bea's and my job, and I didn't have time for my family, friends, or anything outside of work. I would literally get off work, come home, and then start work. Blood pressure and other health-related problems affected me. I was praying one night, and God said, "Look, you got a decision to make. Either you're going to have this job, or you're going to trust Me and do what I've instructed you to do for a long time and run this business. You asked me to increase your territory, right? We can't do that on the job. But we can do it through business. You have to choose." That's when I made up my mind. I said, "Okay, we're going to jump off the ledge." In October 2021, right after purchasing a new home, I turned in my letter of resignation."

But you have what it takes to be one of those Southern cooking greats. You have the energy and the personality, and I'm excited to be a part of your journey. But with food, it's like you make it and the people will come. What made you decide to start networking?

The funny thing about networking is that in my previous profession as an educational fundraiser, I had to network all the time. I'd go into a party and work that room like nobody's business! It was a learned skill and was challenging for me because I'm an introvert, and I don't like networking. I don't like big gatherings. I don't like any of that. I would always have a little panic attack before I got in the room. Then I would pull it together and be like, "Okay, let's do this." I had to put my big girl face on, and I would go into the room and work. Because I had to do it for my job, I never concentrated or put any effort into it in my personal life. I figured, "It'll happen." My last supervisor was a fantastic networker. She knew everybody, and everybody knew her. I envied that. I said, "Man, I really need to step out and start doing some of that." But again, being an introvert and having social anxiety, I pushed it to the side. Then I met you, and you said, "You got to be Drastic! You got to show up! You got to get out there!" I said, "Yeah, do it."

Virtual networking has become more popular since the pandemic. What tips can you share to help people to maximize their virtual networking?

For me, it's like you say, showing up and going to the events. That's the first step; you've got to be in the room. Then be open. When they put you in those little breakout rooms, and you meet people, be open to learning more about them. It's not always about what you can get out of them. It's what you can pour into the people that you're meeting. It's not about making a sale. Maybe that will happen down the line. It's about talking to people, understanding their business, and seeing how you can be of assistance. That's what I find is most successful.

Honestly, networking is not about you. In my community, you all, my coaching clients, have learned to network for each other and bring each other leads. When you do that, they, in turn, will do the same for you. I get it, you have a passion. You have a why, but you could've stayed on your job. What is your key driving force in becoming an entrepreneur?

For me, it was kind of twofold. It was building generational wealth and establishing a legacy. As you know, I love my grandma. Sweet Granny Bea's is named for her. Her name was Beatrice. I'm also a Beatrice. Beatrice is a legacy name in our family. My daughter's middle name is Beatrice. My granddaughter's middle name is Beatrice. Along with that, I want to build generational wealth. I come from a background where when people died everybody came together to cover the expenses because they didn't have insurance. Now my grandmother, bless her heart, had set everything set up. She had final burial expenses paid for, so when she passed, all we had to do was make a few choices. Aside from that, there was not much to pass on.

I've been the first of many things in my family. I was the first to go to and graduate from college, the first to get a graduate degree, and so on. I want to be among the first to establish that legacy of having generational wealth and something to pass on to our children and our children's children. I'm not talking about monetary items. That means passing on knowledge, spiritual wealth, and emotional wealth. I knew entrepreneurship could help me accomplish that goal. That's why I chose it. The other part is I've been entrepreneurial for as long as I can remember. When I was a little kid, I sold cookies. I went door to door asking people if they wanted to buy cookies. I would do a lot of different things. I've always been a little hustler, and it's grown and grown. I've had four businesses since becoming an adult. Each one taught me a lesson and helped me to get further and further. Sweet Granny Bea's has been the most successful to date.

I love all you said about the legacy. Many people miss that part. I love that you want to build a legacy for Zaria, right? Your granddaughter, Zaria.

My daughter is Zaria. Airaz is my granddaughter.

Airaz, Zaria backwards. You want Airaz to feel about you the way you feel about your granny. This is the beginning of that, right? I'm sure you're going to have her in the kitchen working in the business as well. Let's

go back to networking. Tell me about a time that you didn't want to show up, but you did anyway, and you are glad you did.

Honestly, you had a conference, and I didn't want to come. I didn't want to come because I was busy. I had stopped working, and I was trying to figure out how I was going to pay this new mortgage! That was all I was thinking about, and the conference was a distraction. I was like, "Ugh, okay. I'm going to go." Oh, my God, I'm glad I did, because networking is a snowball effect. You meet one person who takes you in a direction, but then they introduce you to other people. Then you keep meeting all these people. Especially when you've been praying and asking for things. I consistently pray to God for the resources, the people, and the know-how to reach my goal and realize my vision. When you network, you see the manifestation. I've been praying for the resources and the people, and I keep meeting people. It's like, "Oh, you want to do videos? I know how to do videos. Oh, you want to do courses? I know how to do courses," or "I know somebody that knows how to do courses," or "You want to have a cooking show? I know somebody that does shows who is a producer. You want to meet them?" You keep meeting people. They're all trying to help you.

That's the power of networking, and everybody wants to help.

Yes, they do. It's not always about spending money. Sometimes, a person will show you. They'll give you a guide or sign you up for a program. They might say, "I know how to do this. I can help you do this quickly. Let's spend 15 minutes together. "It snowballs, and you get everything you need that you've been asking for. But you are building relationships, and you're giving back to others as well. It's like a give and take. You're giving and pouring into people, and they're pouring into you. It's building these relationships, and that's how you move forward.

You already told me you're an introvert. You've had challenges with networking, but let's be specific. What challenges do you have with your personal networking?

The biggest challenge I have is finding the time to do it. I must make the time. I must be intentional about having meetings and going to events, where I can meet more people. We're entrepreneurs, and we're always working. It's saying, "Okay, I intentionally have to stop working in the business, and do this to work on the business so we can grow." It's helping my business grow but in a different way. It's finding the time and being intentional about networking and continuously meeting people.

Tell me about a time that networking made a big difference in your business.

Meeting you, that's huge. I met you because of my commercial realtor. We were talking one day, and she said, "Oh, you've got to meet Toni Harris Taylor." I asked, "Who is that?" She said, "Oh my God, she's a coach. She's this and that. She networks." She connected us and I reached out and followed up. Just meeting you and how that has snowballed with you becoming my coach and opening your network to us. Another instance was meeting another one of your clients. She encouraged me to think about my business in ways that I never would've thought about. Networking with her helped me to be more open to new ways to potentially grow my business. I was open to what she was saying and really listened instead of immediately shooting her ideas down. Had I been closed-minded, I would have missed out on some great ideas. Thank you for bringing that into my life.

It started with Cheryl. I don't know how you met Cheryl. But Cheryl introduced you to me. You and others invested in yourself. You're in the same group. I demanded you all have one-to-ones. When she came into town, you guys had a two-hour one-to-one. I know she poured into you, and you poured into her. It was amazing. My legacy is to leave a group of Drastic Steppers on this planet who are connected forever. Social media is a form of networking. How has social media helped you grow your business?

Social media has probably been one of the most important factors in growing my business today because it's a major way that I engage with my customers. Our primary mode of selling is through farmer's markets, festivals, and shows, and I meet hundreds and thousands of people throughout the year. The only way or one of the biggest ways I can connect with them is through social media. We post, and that's how we've grown our followers. They know about all the new things we're doing now. When they see me at the shows, they're like, "Oh, you got your videos coming. Let me know about that because I want to tune in. Are you going to be cooking? Are you going to open a restaurant?" They get really excited to learn more about what we have and what we're doing. Some of them are on a journey with me because some have been with me since I began. They say things like, "I'm proud of you.

I remember when... " It's great. Social media is extremely important in our business.

This probably goes into the next question as well. What mistakes have you seen entrepreneurs make when it comes to networking? What tips would you give an entrepreneur when it comes to networking?

The biggest mistake would be to go into networking thinking that you must make a sale when you first talk to a new person. That's the greatest mistake. Really taking the time to get to know whom you're talking with and how you can connect on a greater level should be the focus. You must realize you may not get a sale right now, but maybe later down the line and that's okay. Also, you may not sell to that person. Maybe it'll be someone they refer you to. That would be even greater than the sale you may have received from the original person. It's about being genuine and getting to know the person, getting to know their business, and finding out how you can help each other.

You know my saying is, "Show up, be up, follow up to blow up." What does show up mean to you?

To show up is one, seeking opportunities and going. You've must go. If it's virtual, if it's in person, you must go. You never know whom you're going to meet. We're always busy. There's always an excuse but make a commitment to be there. Once you're there, connect with people. Do something. Don't just say, "Oh, this was nice," and then leave. Connect with people. I invited a person to our NIA meeting, to the last one. She's super busy, but she said, "You know what? I'm going to go." I invited her because I wanted her to meet you. We were talking, and she told me that she was being interviewed, and the news outlet was there, and they told her she needed a style coach. I said, "Nikki's a style coach. You've got to meet her. Come on. She's fantastic." She was talking with her and ended up connecting with three or four other people. She said, "This was awesome." It elated me that she was enjoying the experience. You never know. If she hadn't come, and she was a half hour late, and I didn't think she was coming, she would have never made those connections. But she made it. She showed up.

What's your best strategy for follow-up?

My best strategy for following up, honestly, is to get the meeting on the calendar. You helped me learn to stop taking business cards. I don't do it anymore. If somebody wants to meet, they would say, "Well, we should get together." Now I say, "Okay, let's get the calendar out now. Let's do it now. Because if it doesn't happen now, it's not going to happen, because I know me. I get that card, and I won't call." Now, I'm immediate with it. If someone asks to connect, we do it on the spot. Then it's done, and we don't have to worry about it, and we know it's going to happen. That's the most important thing for me.

Describe how your networking has gone viral.

How has my networking gone viral? I would say that with the snowball effect and the continuation. It's so phenomenal because you can be talking to a person, and you don't know what will happen. Like with Rhonda, we were talking to each other about something different, or we thought we were going to connect on something different, and we started talking about real estate and

Airbnbs. She said, "Oh, well, I'm doing that." I said, "I'm doing it too. Well, let's do it together." It didn't have anything to do with what we initially were going to talk about, and it snowballed, because you keep finding out more information. Now I have a partner in real estate I can talk to and bounce ideas off of or work with. But then they have opportunities with Sweet Granny Bea's as well. I've met many people who want to help me. Whether it's for a location or event or catering, they want to help and refer people. It keeps going. That's what makes it viral to me. It keeps going. There are no ends or limits to it.

What's your favorite quote about networking or connecting?

I have a couple of quotes that I love. One is by Peter Gale, which is, "Your network is your net worth." I believe that. But then the other one is Zig Zigler, and he said, "You can have everything in life you want if you will just help enough other people get what they want." I believe that. The more you give, the more you get. That's why I tell people all the time, even with money, it's a flow. Money is a tool. If you keep your hand open, it's going to flow in and out. God has a way of making sure you have what you need that you can continue to help other people. What you put out comes back to you.

What final thoughts can you offer to entrepreneurs who are hesitant to network?

Get out there and get it done. Do it, do it, do it, because it is going to change your life drastically.

DEBRA FIELD: PARENTING COACH

DEBRA FIELD is a parenting coach at Conscious Parent Blueprints. Her passion is partnering with parents to make raising their children fun, easy, and enjoyable. Debra is a highly-rated inspirational speaker with 5+ years of experience as a parenting coach and group facilitator. Debra works with individuals, groups, and organizations to deepen their connection and communication with their children. Her signature program is "The 5 C's to Parenting with Ease" which is a blueprint that can lead to being the parent your heart longs to be.

PHONE: 615.957.4819

WEBSITE: ConsciousParentBlueprints.com

EMAIL: DebraField4@gmail.com

For my husband, who never got to father his own children, but became a father to mine. Thank you for continuing to encourage me when I wanted to give up my entrepreneurial journey.

I have today a guest and an author today in the *Viral Networking for Drastic Results* book, Mrs. Debra Field. Tell us, who are you and what do you do?

I'm Debra Field, the founder, and CEO of Conscious Parent Blueprints. I specialize in partnering with parents to draft family blueprints using proven techniques that will restore their family peace. Parents don't have to continue to live frustrated and embarrassed because of their children's sassiness and acting out at home and school. My passion is working with parents to expand their consciousness, build a plan, and parent with ease. When working with me, parents learn how to calm themselves so they can console their children, connect deeply with them so they can communicate easily, and become much more comfortable with their children and improve their conduct and cooperation.

That's a big deal in a very technology-driven world. Parents are working. Kids are all over the place. That's an important business that you are in. Tell me a little about your story and how you came to make this a business.

I walked through what I teach others now. My story began one morning. I'm a nurse by trade, my first career. I had worked all night. I came in, and was tired, and exhausted. My one-year-old and my three-year-old were tugging at me, wanting my attention. All I could think about was let's get breakfast done, and get to the daycare so I can get some sleep.

When we sat down to eat breakfast, my three-year-old reached across the table and spilled his milk. All I could think of was this is another thing for me to have to do, and I didn't want to do it. I became really angry, and I pushed him; I pushed him harder than I meant to. When I saw big crocodile tears in his eyes, I said, "My gosh, what am I doing?" I grew up in an abusive home, and I had always said I wasn't going to do that to my children. For most of my life, I focused my parenting on doing the opposite of what my parents did. I reached out to a friend about what I was struggling with, and the friend introduced me to some help to deal with parenting and learn more about parenting. I learned a lot about it. I learned I couldn't give apples if I only had oranges. Through the process, I learned how to be there emotionally for my children and how to connect deeply. I learned how to communicate on their level and what appropriate expectations were for them at whatever age they were. Before that, I always thought they were little adults; and they should behave as adults and be like adults, and they were punished if they weren't. Through learning what were normal behaviors and how I could respond in healthy ways and learning about being a total parent, not just physical guidance in their lives, made all the difference in the world for me and my children. We grew much closer, and they were much more well-behaved.

I learned the difference between punishment and discipline. That's a big deal. What I had done to my son was punishment. What I needed was to help him clean it up, and show him how to correct his mistake, and that would have been loving discipline. That would have been teaching and guiding. That's my story of how I came to be a parenting coach.

I love that you took your pain, your mess, and you turned it into something where you could help others because you feel the same pain. I know you really want to see that cycle broken. The other thing I heard in your story is you had to get help. You couldn't do it on your own because you couldn't see what was happening.

I think many of us parents unintentionally adversely affect our children because we don't even know we're doing it.

We don't know what we don't know. You mentioned you were raised in an abusive home, and that's all you knew.

You knew you didn't want to repeat the cycle, but you felt it was coming back up for you, and you asked for help, which is key. You also asked for help to grow your business by getting into my coaching program.

Absolutely. Joining your program is one of the best things I've done. I really like your program, and it breaks it down simply and step-by-step. It is easy to follow and understand.

I didn't solicit that, but thank you for the genuine feedback. One thing I speak to groups about is networking. I met you because you heard me speak. You showed up at an event, and then you said, "I'm in." You came to the Viral Networking Conference. Was that the beginning of your networking, or have you always been networking for business?

A little backstory is as a young child, I was burned on over 90% of my body. People were never nice to me. Being around people was a big fear for me. Networking has been one of the biggest hurdles for me to overcome in my business because I have to put myself out there. I have to find my voice. I have to stand and let people know that I know what I know. That's been one of the biggest struggles, getting out there and networking and meeting new people and standing in my own power. I listened to you do a program for SCORE. I thought *I need her*. I need support in networking, and I need to learn how to do it successfully. I was doing it somewhat prior to that, but I wasn't really speaking in my voice. I wasn't standing out with my business.

Is it safe to say you hated networking, or it was just uncomfortable?

I was very terrified of networking. I was terrified of people. I was really scared of people.

Are you getting more comfortable?

Oh, absolutely. Absolutely, yes.

I love that about our community because they're drastic. All of them are drastic. It happens to be all women. I don't only work with women. It happens to be all women. But it becomes a sisterhood, would you agree?

It is, absolutely. It's like one big family. Now, when questions and issues come up, I put them in our Facebook group, and the members help me with my challenges.

Virtual networking, because of the pandemic, has become much more popular. What tips do you have for someone who is networking virtually?

When you engage with someone at the event, ask a question. That's usually the best way to get them to engage with you and to talk back with you and take the conversation from there. Lead with a question.

I don't think you learned that from me because I don't know that I taught that. But I love that because people love to talk about themselves. The first one to ask a question wins because you get the other person to start talking. Virtually, especially if you get into breakout rooms, that's a great way to get people to engage with you. I know your driving force toward becoming an entrepreneur was your past, the story you told earlier. You could take that same passion and get a job, right?

I did nursing for 28 years and loved it.

However, entrepreneurship is not easy, right?

No, not at all. I have one phrase that keeps me going sometimes when it's that really difficult time. I say, "I can do hard things. I can do hard things."

I can do hard things. You know what I would add to that? If someone else can do hard things, so can I. Because we're not the first ones to create anything here. If other people can do it, then why can't I? They are no more special than me, right? What's your key driving force to staying an entrepreneur, especially when things get hard?

Improving our world through happy children. I feel if we can give our children a happy foundation, from gestation to seven years old, we can get to deeper parenting. At that level, we successfully build our children's confidence, self-worth, and self-esteem. This will make them, and they feel safe in the world, and they can make it a better world. Our world will become better.

One parent, one child at a time, one family. Tell me about a time you didn't really want to show up, and you pushed ahead, and you're glad you did.

Going to the Viral Networking Conference. I knew I needed it, but I didn't want to because I was afraid. I finally said, "Okay, this is a safe place to push through."

The annual Viral Networking Conference is in November. I'm not sure when you're going to read this, but regardless you can go to TheViralNetworkingConference.com and see the content for the next upcoming conference. It was life-changing, not only for those who are in the coaching program, but many are still benefiting. I'm getting messages, and I'm seeing them partnering with people online. It's a beautiful thing. We must show up

when we don't feel like it. That's the best time to show up because something magical happens when you show up and you don't feel like it.

It's like you get a reward. It really is.

Yes. You get a reward. God gives us a medal for showing up. You meet that person who can change your business. You meet your next friend, partner, collaboration, a referral. Something happens, especially when you show up and you don't feel like it every time! I got to get you to Houston. You already said, "I want to move to Houston."

I never thought I would want to move to Texas, but this sisterhood makes me want to.

I know you're a caregiver too in your journey as an entrepreneur, which makes it 10 times harder to be an entrepreneur. My hat is off to you. What other challenges do you have? Now that you've shown up and you're in the event, then what? What other challenges have you had when it comes to turning those contacts into client or referral sources?

Developing the content, actually sitting down and writing out the content. Thanks to the sisterhood, we have Val Vick there now who can help us, we can reach out to, for copywriting and that kind of thing.

How does content fit into networking; the audience may ask? When you go to a networking event, and you put a business card in someone's hand, they are not ready to refer you or do business with you in that instant. Content keeps you connected to those people, and it reminds them to refer you to people in their network. Content is probably one of the most neglected pieces of networking.

It's doing those follow-ups with emails and things like that, reaching out, sending a postcard--the old-fashioned little postcard that says, "I really enjoyed it, thank you," or something memorable from the meeting.

Social media is a form of networking. You've been stretching yourself in social media, and I really admire you and congratulate you for being drastic. You did a whole video challenge, which was uncomfortable for you. I want to congratulate you for being drastic. How has social media helped you? Even though I know you're just now getting momentum on social media, how has social media helped you with your business?

I've met some good friends through our group. The thing is, you broke networking down into such simple strategies. When I think of it, I don't think of it as only business. It's about finding people and making friends and finding out who they are and how they got where they are and what their life is about. To me, it made it much easier to think of it as building friendships.

On social media, you may see somebody, you can connect with and you take those conversations offline by, inviting them to a Zoom chat. You can send a message that says, "Hey, I see you online. Let's hop on Zoom and see what you're up to. I'll share what I'm up to, and let's see how we can help each other."

Yes, a little coffee chat.

I saw a post the other day on Facebook that said, "Stop doing coffee chats and start doing sales calls." I really had to come back and evaluate what I teach, because I teach the coffee chat. It made me pause and say, is that really the case? Should people not be doing coffee chats?

I think when we're serving others, we won't have to worry about our needs being met. If we're building friendships and serving and being there for others, we won't have to worry about a sales call.

Thank you. Plus, with sales calls, people are not open and receptive to you picking up the phone and trying to sell them something. But people are open and receptive to *let's just get to know each other.* Often my coffee chats convert into NIA members or coaching clients because I'm going to tell them who I am and what I do. If I lead with, "I want to sell you something," people aren't attracted to that. The coffee chats take the pressure off. People are not going to want to meet with you if they think you're going to try to sell them something.

They really need to get to know us and see what we're about to trust us enough to join our programs or purchase our products. They must trust us to guide them with their precious children or their business.

Thank you for confirming that I'm still on the right track. What mistakes have you seen entrepreneurs make when it comes to networking?

Just passing out business cards and collecting business cards. It's better to have, as you say, our phones in our hands and ask them, "Hey, when's a good time that we could get together to really talk and get to know each other?" Go ahead and get it on the calendar.

That's right. Get it on the calendar. When you book a date with somebody, it can move. What's interesting is I got called on the carpet for that recently. I met somebody, and I had to go, and she wouldn't let me go without booking a date on her calendar. This was somebody I had met

brand new. She didn't know that was my philosophy already. When she insisted, I was like, "Yep, you are absolutely right. Get it on the calendar." I paused and got it on the calendar. I agree, the biggest mistake is that they take these business cards, and nothing happens. They don't call you. You don't call them. Yes, getting it on the calendar is a consistent theme. Do it! Besides booking appointments on the calendar, give me another networking tip that you have found to work.

Know what you're looking for when you go to the networking event. Be really clear about your niche and who your clients are. Go intending to learn something. Know what it's about. Go with an intention of bringing something back. If it's meeting three people, or if it's meeting one person, know your purpose in going.

Excellent. Know your target market. Many people hate networking because they're not networking in the right places. Know your niche, where they are, and whether they can afford you. When I say, "show up," what does that mean for you?

Go. I'm going to put it simply. Just go. Be there. Go!

Absolutely. It's more than just going. Yes, show up! But if the event is virtual, fix your hair, fix your face, put your earrings on and turn on your camera!

Well, to me that was the show up part. The be up is dressing and getting your energy up and looking good.

Yes, they go hand in hand, for sure. Just go, and don't talk yourself out of going. Many people talk themselves out of going, and they miss out on their blessings. What's your second best strategy to follow up?

For me, it's to have follow-up emails on my calendar that way I can fill them right in. I've got it on my calendar, and I've got it ready. Many people will have emails scheduled to automatically go out. I like to make them a little more personal and really connect with that person.

Very good. I know you're in the infancy, to use a child term, of your networking and being a part of my community, but describe up to now how your networking has gone viral.

Well, I'll be honest. My calendar has been pretty full. I've met with many networking people, done one-on-one calls, and got to know everybody. This is my work week, but it's fun. It's really been fun.

Because you're also a Network in Action member, suffice it to say that you are networking now more than you ever have. I introduced you to another networking group that's focused on speakers. One of the things about coaching with me and networking with me is I share all the networks I know of. I'm teaching you techniques, but what good is it if you never go to any events? I introduced Debra to a great network where she will be able to get on podcasts and be able to share her expertise about parenting there. What's your favorite quote for business and networking?

My quote for my business is, "Change the world by changing your parenting." I really believe we can change the world if we can change that. But networking? Build friendships. If I really had to say something, build friendships and let the rest take care of itself.

I have a client who said, "I don't need more friends." Now, she is an advocate for friendship through

networking and how it changes the game. What final thoughts would you offer entrepreneurs who are hesitant to network?

If you want your business to be successful, you must network, period.

ANDREA HANCOCK: PROFESSIONAL ORGANIZER

ANDREA HANCOCK believes that an organized life can significantly decrease stress in an inevitably stressful life. Since 2010 she's been an active member of NAPO (National Association of Productivity and Organizing Professionals). She works with her team to help Dexterous Organizing's clients to work from strategy, implementation, and (for those who are open to creating positive change) organizing coaching. They also handle relocation management for those in the Washington, DC Metropolitan area.

PHONE: 703.653.0088

WEBSITE: DexterousOrganizing.com

EMAIL: Team@DexterousOrganizing.com

I dedicate this book to all who choose to fill me up and build me up to be better than I thought possible. You inspire me to do that for others.

Andrea owns Dexterous Organizing. In your own words, tell everybody who you are and what you do.

I am Andrea Hancock with Dexterous Organizing, and what we do helps reduce stress and save time for our clients. How do we do that? We help busy professionals, busy people, and families in the DC Metro Area, and soon to be around the country, with transitions. It's stressful and overwhelming for people to deal with transitions in life. It's the mundane tasks and the lack of organization that add to the stress on top of everything else a person must take care of in life. We also organize people's spaces, from a small room to every room in their house, as well as help with their relocation management needs. We help save people time, and money, avoid unnecessary stress and give them calm and peace and focus and control; everything people really crave these days.

I love that she's also a coaching client and we've been working on her market dominating position. Tell me about the pets and how they play into this. I love that and I'm not even a pet person.

If you are familiar with Northern Virginia, especially Alexandria, you're going to see pet owners, and people walking their dogs. I've even seen people walking their cats! People here love their animals. You can't walk very far in Old Town Alexandria without hitting a pet boutique, or a dog salon, and also the Doggie Daycares. People love their animals here. And guess what? Our Dexterous Organizing team loves animals. Most of us have a dog or a cat. I also have a turtle and some fish. I love cats. I love dogs. It's just a perk for us when we get to go help our clients in their spaces and organize, and there is a lovely cat or dog there that we can also dote on.

You also help the families prep the pet for moving. That's a big deal. The pets get traumatized. It's new for them too. By the way, she has a dog named Duncan. Who ever heard of that? How did you get into the organizing business?

I wanted to be an entrepreneur for a while. I was in an entrepreneurship club in college. In fact, in my yearbook, they have superlatives. I was voted most likely to be a businessperson in high school. I didn't know exactly what I wanted to do. I had an accounting degree. I loved accounting, but I wasn't passionate enough to open a business in accounting. Then I was watching the television show, *Clean House with Niecy Nash*, the black woman with the flower in her hair. She would talk about mayhem. She would help people. She was the coach in the show. Then they had the interior designer, and they had a yard sale guy, to sell all the clutter. They also had a professional organizer on the show…for the first few seasons; her name was Linda Koopersmith. I didn't know there was such a thing. I investigated it. I Googled it, and then I found NAPO, which is the National Association of Productivity and Organizing Professionals, NAPO.net. There's a national organization, and throughout the country there are chapters. I joined them at the national level, then I joined the Washington, DC chapter. I found my peeps, and that was in 2010. In 2011, I went to my first NAPO conference in San Diego and saw that this was an industry for me.

What made you start networking?

When I think about how I started organizing, it was through a network. I joined NAPO at the national level, but when I joined the chapter, the women there, were open. There were a few guys, but it was mostly women. They were helpful in starting the business. We viewed ourselves as friendly competitors. There's enough business out here for all of us. They helped me think about books to read and showed me the ropes. A lot of times with new organizers, they hire each other as subcontractors. That allowed me to see what it was like, to be on the job, so to speak, and it helped me to realize what clients I really wanted to serve.

When it comes to networking, there are many emotions. Some love it. Some hate it. Where do you fall on the love-hate meter when it comes to networking?

I love it. I had to realize how to network the right way. I was a member of Business Networking International for a while. If anything, it taught me how to speak in front of people. At my first few meetings, I was nervous, and it was interesting. We already talked about being spiritual sisters. We're used to talking to people all the time in our ministry. But it was different. When we're talking about our God, it's different from when we're talking about business and people. If people reject Him, that's fine. But if people reject me and my business and what I'm saying, who I am, and my business is my baby, then it is hard. Networking regularly helped me to articulate who I am, and what I was looking for, and think about, again, who my target market is so that I could formulate those things and articulate them well. Then it taught me how to network because a lot of them are business professionals and business owners. I would see on their desks, stacks, and stacks of business cards over the years. It taught me, "What are you going to do with those cards?" Having one-to-ones, and building relationships is what networking's about. When I realized I will not go here and pick up a bunch of cards and end up throwing them in the trash, I'm going to get one or two cards. If I got one, I know you are a proponent of three, but if I even got one one-to-ones out of it. I felt like it was a more productive meeting.

You said something important, and that is when we are networking for our own business, it's our baby. If people aren't interested in our baby, it's like telling

us our baby is ugly and who wants to hear that? When you show up, and especially when you are a part of a networking organization like Network In Action, where people are there to help you grow, you put your defenses down and it helps you to show up for your business. Virtual networking has become more popular since the pandemic. What tips can you share to maximize virtual networking?

I'm now a member of NIA, and I love that virtual networking started picking up during the pandemic. Most of the chapters are virtual. The app is there; the technology is there. It is helpful in helping us to network virtually. I did get burned out once. It was about 2014; I was going here and there and doing one-to-ones, and going to network events. I was chapter president of this organization and doing this and doing that. A lot of it required traveling. Get in the car, deal with traffic, and find parking. Here's a trick of the trade. When you are the one doing the one-to-one, you can say, "Meet me at the Panera." Everybody can meet you at Panera. You sit there until 4 p.m. and get them all out of the way. But now, with virtual, you don't have to go anywhere, and people can join your Zoom room. I can now network with people further away than my local area. This has helped me think about adding revenue streams outside of helping people in the DMV area.

Virtual networking is not going away. In fact, for me, and I know for a lot of my clients, virtual networking was a gift from the pandemic because it got us thinking about how to grow our business outside the four walls of where we live. Like you said, now you are thinking about how to maximize video and use other strategies to attract people to your business. I still think there's a great

place for in-person networking. In fact, two of my NIA groups are in-person and I love the energy of the people in the room. What I don't want is for people to discount virtual. I still have people in my network who say, "I hate virtual networking." They don't see the gift in it. It is such a gift, but you must do it right. Otherwise, it's a waste of time. I know you said that when you were in high school, they voted you number one to be a business owner. Entrepreneurship is not easy. What's your driving force to staying an entrepreneur?

I think one of my strengths is also a weakness and that is I'm stubborn. I won't give up. It's a strength and a weakness. It's a strength when it comes to being an entrepreneur. One thing I didn't love about being an employee is—I'm not a genius, but I'm not stupid. I felt the hierarchy and all the corporate red tape around certain things, which is stupid to me. I even now, to this day, I tell my team, "You have an idea, you express it." One thing that I love about entrepreneurship is, I'm able to maximize my skill set, and things that I'm not great at, learn how to delegate them. In a service-based business, sometimes when I think I can't do this anymore, I want to quit. Then, I get a text message, or I get a review or I get something from a client that says, "You are gifted at this. This is something that helped me change my life. You helped me in a dark spot. I didn't know how I was going to get through this. That is a reward in itself, even past monetary significance.

Tell me about a time you didn't want to show up, you pushed ahead and you're glad you did.

Let's talk about when I met you. I'm involved in an organization, and they have monthly meetings, but they meet in the evening, virtually. I'm in a role now in my business where I'm CEO, in meetings all day, and I'm at my computer. By the evening, I want a glass of wine. I want to eat dinner with my husband. I want to watch a show and call it a day. The night before, I was in a meeting for organizers, and then this one showed up on my calendar and your marketing was great. It was Build a Six-Figure Business. I'm like, "I'm already there, and beyond. Let me hear more about how to succeed." I said, "I'm not going to have my camera on. I'm just going to show up." And then when you mentioned you were a Jehovah's Witness, I was like, "Ah, and we started texting." I just started typing it in and we connected. Like you said, I've met many people through you. I went to Houston, Texas for your conference, and met many great people. Now I'm in your coaching program. I'm looking forward to drastic results in my business. I showed up.

I'm excited that you showed up too. Look at us now. I'm grateful that you pushed through, not only for myself but for you, because I'm seeing you blossom through my network as well. Even though you like or love networking, what challenges do you have when it comes to networking?

Networking takes time. Another thing is, regardless of what people think, I'm an introvert. People drain my energy. I need a lot of alone time to recharge. What could happen with networking is, if I don't set boundaries around how many one-to-ones I have in the day or the week, I can be a grumpy mumpy by the end of the week. What I learned is, do what I can reasonably do. That's one reason I love NIA. We have monthly meetings. It's not a weekly commitment. That gives me more time for one-to-ones. One thing I love about entrepreneurship is flexibility. It's hectic, but you can have some flexibility there. It could be a double-edged sword, though. With flexibility, you can overextend yourself. Then you could have back-to-back-to-back-to-back meetings. I try to set boundaries around how many meetings I'll have in a day, or how many meetings I'll have in a week. It could be tough because that might mean my slots fill up quickly. If you're doing two to three networking meetings a week and you're trying to book two to three one-to-ones from those meetings, that's exponential.

Time is a challenge for all of us and you're right. It can get out of control, and you'll spend all your time networking and not doing business. Balance is key to that. Tell me about a time when networking made a big difference in your business.

I look at networking as a box of chocolates, like Forrest Gump says, you never know what you're going to get. I also look at it as a long game. Sometimes when I find myself in opportunities or I find myself with certain clients, I really sit and think, *where did this come from?* If I do the connections, and they came from a networking event or networking opportunity, they were never from the first pebble in the pond, so to speak. It was I met this person. We had a one-to-one. They connected me with this person and then I had a one-to-one. Then it connected me to this organization. That organization connected me to this opportunity. I've been in the *Washington Post* a few times, and as far as being quoted or an article about my business and many other opportunities, when I look back through how those came about, it was through networking.

I'm telling you everything that I have in my life, even my husband came through networking. Networking changes the game, but it starts with, you got to be there. Now social media is a form of networking. How has social media helped you with your business?

We've got clients through social media, primarily Facebook and Instagram. We always ask, how did you hear about us? I also feel that if I meet somebody and I'm not ready to either engage with them in business or have a one-to-one, I'll follow them on social media. It keeps them in front of me. I get to spy on them a little. If I'm doing that, guess what? Other people are too. Our social media is a way for people to get introduced to Dexterous Organizing, get introduced to me, and stay in front and top of mind because social media is good at what it does. They want people always looking at their screens. The more you put content out there, the more people are going to see you. It could be an instance where you want to refer somebody and you say to yourself, *I remember their business name, their first name.* You go to social media and start typing it in, and boom. Then you can send that, or people can refer you through your social media.

Social media changed the game for me. I never even wanted to be on social media. Then I was pushed. But now, my business has changed drastically. I think that's how you found out about my conference, through social media. The point is this: people might not be ready to buy from you the day they meet you. It's critical that you stay connected to them. It is not up to them to remember you. It's up to you to keep yourself in front of them, and social media helps us to do that. What mistakes have you seen entrepreneurs make when it comes to

networking? What is your best networking tip to alleviate those mistakes?

One thing I hate is when I feel like I'm getting sold to. I love networking for collaboration. I love networking for thinking about how I can help others. I try not to leave a networking one-to-one without thinking about someone I can introduce them to, or thinking about an event they can come to, because, again, if they meet this person and they meet that person, who knows down the line what opportunities can come from that? I don't want to be single-minded or shortsighted to say, "Oh, you need my services." That would be pushy, or it could be a turn off. I think of networking as an opportunity to connect and then we'll see where it goes from there, no pressure. I've had opportunities where people I've networked with became my clients, but it wasn't necessarily the first top of my goal.

The challenge or the mistake is being too pushy. You turn people off when you are pushy and desperate. The other thing is, when they sit down with you in a one-to-one, when you describe who you are and what you do well, they will recognize if they need your services or not. You don't even have to ask. They'll say, "Oh yeah, I need that." That's your opening. It's all about whom you know and helping to connect with each other. What does it mean to show up?

To show up can be difficult. As I mentioned before, if I've overbooked myself, as an introvert, I can have low energy. One thing that helps me show up I discovered in a book I read years ago when I first started my business. It changed the game for me as far as networking. The book was, *How to Win Friends and Influence People* by Dale Carnegie. It said people will like you if you listen to them. Sometimes when I'm low energy, I ask questions. I get to know more about the other person. I mean, don't ask questions to be disengaged. I don't have to think about my story or talk too much, which drains my energy, but I can listen. In magical human nature, people are going to like me. People do business with people they know, like, and trust. I experimented with it. Sometimes I've said almost nothing. I listen to a person who likes to talk, or I ask questions to engage a person. At the end of the conversation, they're like, "This was such a good conversation. You are so sweet."

One of the biggest challenges I know is following up on networking. What tips can you offer or what's your best strategy for following up?

The best way I can follow up is by having systems. As an organizer, that's one thing that I realized. I love those things. Years ago, I was an Evernote certified consultant. Evernote is software that helps you capture basically anything. It helps you journal. It helps you take pictures. It helps you recall things. You can search for things. You can find it. They had a component on that software where you could take pictures of cards. I don't know if it still exists because I haven't used Evernote like I used to. But you could capture people's information. You could add them to your contacts and/or connect with them on LinkedIn. I would get a couple of cards at a networking event, but my goal was to capture the people whom I knew I wanted to connect with again and get their information immediately. Then when I was good at it, I would send a card if they have the address, I would send a card, thanking them for meeting them. I would send them an email. That was a way for me to be well known.

Describe how your networking has gone viral.

Through social media. If a person's not going to follow you, follow them. People put their social media on their cards, and if I'm not going to engage them, I follow them on their social media. Usually they follow me back. Then, if you're continually posting and they're continually posting, you find events that they're having that you can go to. Find workshops that they might be hosting, and then you find collaboration opportunities that you wouldn't have known had you not connected with them on social media.

What's your favorite quote about networking or connecting?

My favorite quote is from an African proverb. "If you want to go fast, go alone. If you want to go far, go with others." I've already gone a lot farther than I have ever thought I would with others.

What final thoughts can you offer to entrepreneurs who are hesitant to network?

Do it. Just be like Nike. Learn, then do it enough that you love it. Sometimes we do something enough that we hate it. Find out what works for you. Network the way you would like to network. The bottom line is to make connections, then show up to help others. Go there and think *how I can help somebody else?* It takes the pressure off you. Along the way, people will know and trust you, which in turn will bring you business in the long run. Know that it's a long game. Sometimes you can get a sale at a networking event, but generally, it's a long game.

SEDRIC HUDSON: REAL ESTATE BROKER & AGENT

SEDRIC HUDSON is the Broker/Owner of Harmony Real Estate LLC., a real estate company founded on the principle of creating harmonious relationships in order to build community, experience growth and establishing legacy. Connecting and building relationships with people from all types of backgrounds has become a distinct skill for Sedric. In recent years, Sedric has won the honor of Top Producer and due to his ability to connect on a grand scale, he now operates business in multiple Texas urban centers.

PHONE: 512.736.6803
WEBSITE: BrooksandDavis.com
EMAIL: SHudson@BrooksandDavis.com

I dedicate this chapter to my wife and two sons who support me in every endeavor I pursue. They give me hope, keep me focused, and fuel the engine that drives my determined spirit.

We have another author from the *Viral Networking for Drastic Results* book. Our next author is Sedric Hudson. He is an NIA member. He is also a real estate agent and broker in the Austin and Houston areas. Welcome, Sedric. Let's get a little background on you. Who are you and what do you do?

As previously stated, my name is Sedric Hudson. I'm a realtor located here in Houston, Texas. In addition, I also serve Austin, Texas and the surrounding area. I serve as an associate broker with Brooks and Davis Real Estate Firm. I'm also the Broker/Owner of Harmony Real Estate LLC. As a real estate broker, my job is to grow, educate, and lead both agents and clients through the buying, selling, and investing process.

I know you're big on education because you came from the education sector. How did you go from education to being a real estate agent?

That's a good question. Fate. I've had dreams of being an entrepreneur for years. However, I must say fear and uncertainty gave me cause to pause. Even though I recognized my potential, value, and the many attributes I knew would undoubtedly make me a successful entrepreneur, I was still fearful. After leaving my professional career in education because of a series of bad decisions, what seemed to be a negative event at the time would eventually open doors and quickly turn into a successful full-time entrepreneurial career. Even then, I still had to make the tough decision of committing entirely to entrepreneurship. Ultimately, I realized that I not only had a unique opportunity to rewrite the story of my family's past, but the ability to set an entirely new trajectory for my family's future.

What made you start networking?

I believe I've always been a networker because I have always had an outgoing and social personality. As I've gotten older, I've just become more intentional about how I socialize. There's a saying in the corporate world, "It's not about what you know, it's about who you know." With that in mind, I quickly came to the understanding of how vital and necessary it is to connect with others and tap into resource wells that I otherwise would not have the ability to attain on my own. Connecting, relationship building, and networking are at the core of who I am. It's part of my identity and what I love and enjoy doing. My passion for it and drive towards pursuing it are second to none. I knew that this topic of discussion would come up and I must admit, Toni is the queen of networking! We all know that hands down. I'll give you that. However, I'm looking at things from a completely different perspective. If you're going to be the queen, I'll be the prince. When I think about the idea of networking independently, I know without a doubt that you are sensational at connecting or putting groups of people together. My skill is all about the actual connection, with the person. Don't get me wrong, I'm no guru. I see those as two completely different ideas. One focuses on getting people partnered together and the other focuses on building relationships.

There is a difference between connecting people and connecting with people. Honestly, I have the gift of doing both. You do too. But talk more about connecting with people.

If I had to give an example of what I believe my "superpower" is, I would say that it is the ability to "speak every language in the world." What I mean by that is not that I literally speak every language in the world, but there has not been an individual I've ever come in contact with that I've felt like I could not create a genuine bond, relationship, or connection with. My ability to have a street vocabulary, professional vocabulary, corporate vocabulary, educational vocabulary, and so on allows me to step foot into any room. No matter the size of the crowd, denomination of the people, the origin of the individuals, their ethnic background, or culture, I feel comfortable in any room. Not only do I feel comfortable, but I thrive. It's a skill set I've been blessed with. That's what I mean when I say that I speak every language.

When it comes to networking, there are many emotions. Some people love it. Some people hate it. Where are you on the networking meter?

I'm a firm 10! When it comes to my feelings and opinions about whether someone should be engaged with networking opportunities and their effectiveness, please understand that I am sold out on the idea that networking works. I'm going to continue to say this, it's all about relationship building. The value of what other people bring is something I believe in. I believe in the value of pouring into others. Therefore, I love people and I love networking.

Virtual networking has become popular since the pandemic. What tips can you share with someone about networking virtually?

These are things that have helped me: First and foremost, be creative, open-minded, and intentional. Don't just think outside of the box. I think that people have to think through the box. What I mean by that is that you should approach virtual networking with the understanding that many of the traditional ways of networking will have to change. At the same time, some things can and will remain the same. Thinking outside of the box in order to navigate your way through the challenges that virtual networking brings is essential. What does that look like in reality? Here are a few recommended criteria for success:

Set a goal for a number of follow ups. Recognize that people's time and attention are limited. Most importantly, be cognizant of how you personally add value to others. In other words, know your superpower. I've learned through experience that challenges and roadblocks are typically disguised pathways to new ideas, innovations, and successes. I think if you consider these simple rules, you'll be successful with virtual networking.

What's your driving force to stay an entrepreneur, especially when it gets hard?

There are many things that drive me to stay steadfast and focused. However, there are a couple that stand out above the rest. My company's core values and the inspiration that I get from my wife and kids are undoubtedly the primary driving forces. Harmony Real Estate is all about three things: building community, experiencing growth, and establishing a legacy. That coincides exactly with want I for my family. It's what I want my boys to see that I stand for as they get older. It's what I want them to carry into the next lineage of young people that come after them. Just as important, having a clear vision and knowing that I am in charge of that vision manifesting itself gives me the push that I need when times get hard. Without a doubt, being mindful of these things will not only keep me in entrepreneurship, but allow me to continue to have a relentless pursuit of excellence.

Tell me about a time you didn't want to show up, you pushed ahead, and you're glad you did.

Sometimes that seems like a daily obstacle, doesn't it? There was a time not too long ago a woman named Carla Jean, who was introduced to me by our associate pastor at the church that I attend, invited me to a networking event. Our church was hosting a two-day business workshop on how to grow your business. The church had an event on how to grow a business. It was all wrapped around entrepreneurship. It was perfect. When I was introduced to Carla Jean, it took me a few minutes to regain my clear consciousness because I thought she was just one of those people that would just overwhelm me. She was, let's just say, long-winded, chatty, and it took me a second. One had to step back when you met her. Once she found out that I was in real estate, she insisted I come to a networking event her company was having the next week. Of course, I agreed because I love networking. Once I arrived at the event and spent some time with Carla, I realized my personality was a great fit with hers. I went there with an open mind. I went there with an agenda, being intentional, and ready to make those appointments. When I got there, Carla Jean introduced me to everyone at the networking event. To my surprise, I believe I was the only real estate agent in the room that night. It was a room full of educators and educational representatives. I had been pondering, planning, asking, and seeking, "How can I continue to stay heavily connected with my passion, interest, and career in education as well as continue to do real estate and be an entrepreneur?" Voila, here comes the opportunity. I ended up connecting with the provost of a local junior college in the area. I connected with two grant writing directors at another junior college in the area. One of the most important connections was with the Director of Counseling for a neighboring school district. We hit it off instantly. We scheduled a time to follow up and chat with one another. Sure enough, in the next couple of days, she planned to have me come and speak at one of the school district's alternative campuses to students who were obviously at the alternative school for making poor decisions. The speaking engagement was called "Teachable Tuesdays." It was all about success stories, talking about resilience, perseverance, fighting adversity, and taking negative situations and turning them into positives. I had gained three young male mentees that wanted me to be their mentor. In addition, they wanted to go into the field of real estate. They introduced me to three or four more administrators on the campus. From that point, they made me the go-to person for these Teachable Tuesdays. I bring in other professionals I'm connected with and they are allowed to share their stories. Now I'm going to be holding a first-time homebuyer session for the community of that school district in the near future.

You love networking. I love networking. But there are still challenges in networking, even when you love it. What are your challenges when it comes to networking?

The largest challenge is at times I forget that there isn't always a floodgate on the other side of that mountain waiting to overflow my way. What I mean by that is that there are times I go into networking events with a business need, or a business want where I expect good networking to pay off. It doesn't always happen that way. Again, I believe that networking will always repay itself, repay you tenfold. However, it may not always be on your timing. Aside from that, figuring out what to do with the array of business cards I get at every networking event. I have come up with a strategy and a system for dealing with that.

How has social media networking helped your business?

Let me just tell you, it has been sensational. I must admit that early on I gave resistance to social media networking. But I must say social media, at least in my opinion at the moment, is the ultimate form of networking. Again, let me be clear. As far as I'm concerned, there's still nothing like face-to-face interaction. That's what I prefer, but social media allows us to get our message, our brand, our voice, and our product out to the world in a matter of seconds or minutes. It specifically helped me grow my business because I'm able to do what I do and share it on a grander scale. Whether it's real estate education, promotions, marketing, sales, or transactions, social media has turned my individual efforts into more of an assembly line of information that goes out to the full onion of people. What I mean when I say "onion of people" is it goes out to my sphere of influence, then out to the next person's sphere of influence that shares it, and the next and the next and the next. The message can reach much further than I would've ever been able to do on my own. Social media just creates this world of interconnectedness, which I believe makes us feel like we're all doing life together, which builds a sense of trust and a relationship, which, as we know, is good for business.

What other mistakes have you seen entrepreneurs make when it comes to networking?

This "give me, give me" attitude. For me, it's one of the most disturbing, and quite frankly, annoying, things to deal with at a networking event. That person that wants, wants, wants. The person that only talks and never listens. It's literally almost painful to watch sometimes.

Entrepreneurs attend networking events and come with nothing to offer, no value to add to others. They just want. They only want to talk about themselves, their business, and their goals, and try to figure out whom they can latch onto that will help their business make a million dollars overnight without them doing any other work. These individuals, these entrepreneurs, are missing out on the whole mark and the beauty of networking, which is getting to know people and your community.

One of the most effective networkers that I've ever had the privilege of meeting, outside of Toni, was one of my mentors, a guy by the name of Charles. Charles mentors me in the space of real estate investing. He's quickly become one of the most successful entrepreneurs in the Houston area when it comes to acquiring rental properties with little to no money out of your own pocket. When I first met Charles, I was at a networking event sitting at a table with some guys I brought to the networking event with me. He came up to the table, sat down with us, and immediately asked all of us, "What do you guys do for a living?" We all responded. After everyone responded, I posed the same question to him. I said, "What do you do for a living?" He says, "I help make people money." Initially, I thought to myself, "He's full of himself," because it came off brash. That's why I asked him again, "No, really, what do you do?" He says, "No, really, I help make people money." This time he follows up that response with a few questions that helped him identify what my business needs and goals were, what I did, and what I was looking for. After about an hour or so of talking, I soon learned that his original response to the question of what he did for a living was extremely genuine. Not only was he genuine about it, but he was over the top brilliant when it came to real estate investing and helping people make money. Down the road, we fast forward. I later enrolled in his zero to one real estate investing course, which cost me a pretty penny. But it was worth every dime, in which my mind would completely transform around the concept of investing. My wife and I are in the process right now of buying our first investment home with a goal of 10 in the next two years. Instead of having that "give me" attitude; like Charles, I want to give to you. I want to add value.

What does it mean to show up?

For me, showing up is all about being fully present and engaged in the moment. Walking into the room or virtual space with expectations and bringing your best efforts, for me, reminds me of Tuesday nights. Tuesday nights for us here in my household are swim nights for my two boys. They both absolutely love swim nights. They love going to swim, showing off their skills while they're swimming so mom and dad can see. I'm often saddened, however, when I sit on the other side of that looking glass at swim class because I look around and, to be honest, I see about 75% of the adult parent crowd, they're fully engaged with their phones, not the kids, but their phones. You can see the swim instructors. You can see the kids, every couple of seconds, looking up to see if mom and/or dad are noticing what they're doing. Yes, the parents are there, but they didn't necessarily show up. They're not fully engaged. That's how I remember and how I think about showing up. You're going to be remembered by your showing up and what you do.

What's your best strategy for following up?

For following up, schedule in the moment. I learned that from you. You do it best, you teach it best, you stress it best. I have since adopted that practice, schedule in the moment. Do not wait until you get home or back to your office and try to recall that important conversation that you had or shuffle through the array of business cards, and attempt to decipher which card was from the person you had that great connection with. Utilize whatever scheduling tool you prefer in order to get that done in the moment. I'm simple. As I said before, I use Google calendar. It's great for me because it's color coded. It's set to give me an alarm for my appointments. It's also connected to my family household calendar. The "boss," my wife, she's always quick to give me that additional reminder, if necessary, but schedule it in the moment.

Describe how your networking has gone viral.

In full disclosure, my networking has not gone viral yet. However, I fully believe in the fruits of networking and what it brings. Therefore, I'm in a constant current status of, shall we say, viral networker. I consider this relentless pursuit more like a marathon, since I'm a runner, than a sprint. I have not reached that status yet of viral networker, but I'm on my way.

Let me change your mind. I looked up the word "viral." I also heard someone else say that you are viral when other people are talking about you when you're not in the room. We equate viral to millions of likes or views or whatever. But viral is when someone is saying, "You need to talk to Sedric."

That does change my perception of it then. I'll say I'm 50/50. I'm halfway there because I still want to continue that chase, but it does give but it does give me a new perspective.

What's your favorite quote about networking or connecting?

I've adopted this lately. I read a quote by a lady, Margaret J. Wheatley. She's a bestselling author, speaker, teacher, community worker, and advisor. I closely relate networking to relationship building connectedness, but this is why I latched onto this quote that she wrote. It reads, "Relationships are all there is. Everything in the universe only exists because it is in a relationship with everything else. Nothing exists in isolation. We have to stop pretending we are individuals that can go at it alone." It sticks with me. I like the thought of it because again, it signifies the importance of relationships, doing life together, and growing with each other. I thought it was great.

That's perfect. What final thoughts would you give to entrepreneurs who are hesitant to network?

Here's my tidbit of advice: Your legacy and the legacy of your business will not make their mark on the grounds of the idea that you made it work by yourself, your way. Your legacy and the legacy of your business will be remembered by its sustainability and the impact that it has on other people. Get out there, share your value with other people, and your business, and you will grow.

SONJA LOWE: CEO & LIFE COACH

SONJA LOWE is a visionary entrepreneur, known as the "Embrace Coach." She is an award-winning speaker, author, producer and life and leadership coach. As CEO of Sonja Lowe Enterprises, LLC and Choice 1 Media Group, she coaches entrepreneurs and independent creatives to embrace their authentic self with a media footprint by becoming a credible media personality, creating and producing affordable, professional and engaging digital content that gets them noticed and increases business revenue.

PHONE: 346.229.5815

WEBSITE: SonjaLowe.com

EMAIL: Sonja@SonjaLowe.com

Dedicated to every individual desiring to grow and be a difference maker.

Today, we have another author of the *Viral Networking for Drastic Results book*, and I'm super excited to introduce you to Sonja Lowe, The Embrace Coach. Sonja, like most of us, is a multi-preneur, but the foundation of how she's grown every one of her businesses has been networking. Let me present to you, my friend and landlord, Sonja Lowe. In your words, who are you and what do you do?

Hello, I am Sonja Lowe, The Embrace Coach. I coach entrepreneurs to embrace their media footprint by becoming a persuasive spokesperson, creating and producing professional and affordable digital content that gets you noticed while increasing business revenue.

She's The Embrace Coach. She also has Choice 1 Media Group (C1MG, LLC) Tell us about that.

I am the CEO, award winning executive producer and director of Choice 1 Media Group (C1MG, LLC), a full-service media production company where we produce movies, talk shows, commercials, digital or print media and provide media coaching. I'm also an Amazon Best Selling author, *Becoming Bare – A Guide To Becoming Your Authentic Self* and also the COO of SGA TV Network streaming on Apple TV, Roku, Amazon Fire TV, Google and more. I'm honored to have my very own TV network along with my partner where we can actually cultivate collaborations among independent artists, which entrepreneurs fall in this category, to have a platform that is geared towards them and gives exposure at an affordable price.

We will stop there because there is more, but how did the idea for your businesses come about? Let's start with the Embrace Coach. You have a nursing background. How did you go from nursing to this?

Great question. Nursing is definitely where I started. It was my foundation. I have a heart to serve and embrace others. Most people that know me know I love God, and if you love God, you serve. Serving is who I am not what I do. Becoming a nurse was definitely something I knew I could do to serve and embrace people. I loved nursing, enjoyed doing it, but I knew there was more. I knew that nursing was not where I was supposed to land. It was a stepping stone to where I was going. Nursing taught me how to truly embrace and love people right where they are. It taught me so many life skills. It taught me how to literally take care of the whole person, whether they were healthy or not. Nursing gave me the foundation of really becoming an entrepreneur. I became known as the embracer because I love to hug and accept people for who they are and where they are. When you're on the hospital floor, you have to have integrity to do what you're supposed to do when you're in the rooms. I decided that I wanted to do this and I wanted to do this for myself. Have my own rooms to help others. Of course, the burning desire to have my own company and leave a legacy was always there. My passion was to build something, to help others and hence, birthed entrepreneurship.

What made you start networking?

I was always invited to networking events, but it wasn't until I heard someone tell me that if you start networking, you will build your community, and I went 'build your community?" They said, you will build your tribe who believes in you. I decided to start and I said, okay, I'm going to go. I started going to networking events and loved it because I'm a people person. From then on, I continued to network and networking led me to actually opening up my very first business over 25 years ago, which was totally different from what I'm doing now. But realizing that networking truly was the lifeblood for connections, it brought me to a new relationship that budded a new relationship and so forth and so on.

When it comes to networking, people either love it or they hate it. Where do you fall on the networking meter?

I actually enjoy it. People can tell by my energy that I enjoy networking. I truly love to embrace people. Sometimes it's finding the time and prioritizing the time that's really the most challenging aspect. But as far as where I am on the meter, I absolutely enjoy networking because I love embracing people.

You and I met networking, and you and your partner, Marietta, met networking and it has been transformational, especially when you know how to and learn how to build real connections beyond the business card. Virtual networking has become more popular because of the pandemic and it's not leaving. What tips would you give to someone for virtual networking?

Number one, I would definitely tell them that if you see something that is virtual, take the leap, and just join. I can tell you that virtual allows you to meet people all over the world. You never know who you may connect to. That very next person may be the connection to catapult you and your business to another level. But also, you may be the answered prayer for someone else as well.

Now Sonja, every entrepreneur I've ever met has thought about getting a job, so what is the driving force you have to stay an entrepreneur?

Well, first off you have to know your purpose. You have to know in the pit of your belly what your purpose is. I honestly know that my purpose is to be an entrepreneur not to work for someone else. It boxes me in and I do not like being put in a box. I am a visionary and desire to build a legacy larger than myself and coach others to do the same. Yes, there are times and moments that you want to quit. There are times you're like, forget it, I wouldn't have this headache if I just go work for someone else. But at the end of the day, Toni, I have to always go back to what's my purpose? My purpose is larger than myself to show that if I can do it, you can do it as well. To embrace, coach and believe in other entrepreneurs until they can believe in themselves. I can't build a legacy for my family over there but by building my own, I can build a legacy and leave a legacy for generations to generations as the word of God states.

Tell me about a time you didn't want to show up, you pushed ahead and you're glad you did.

I would have to honestly say that was a few years ago. I went to a particular networking event, I didn't want to, but I pushed and made it there. I didn't see the immediate benefit but, of course, we always want to see the immediate. I didn't see the immediate benefit, but if I rewind and go back to it, if I did not push to go to that networking event that day, I would've never met my partner, Marietta, and hence today I would not have what we're building. I pushed through that day, I did not want to go. I joined and I didn't see the immediate benefit, but I stuck with it because I'm not a quitter. There was a blessing for me in the midst of it all. Now that right there, that's a testimony. The struggle at times is real talk. I would just say, to me when there's a push and there's a struggle, there's a bigger blessing. But we also can accept it and recognize it as the call is larger than you. So, it's all worth it.

I know you love networking, but we all have challenges with it. What are your challenges with networking?

My number one challenge is my schedule. My schedule is crazy. My number one challenge is trying to find the time, knowing that sometimes networking is in the middle of the day. If you're busy you have things that pop off. I'm trying to learn how to take and prioritize and make my networking a priority.

Absolutely, because I know you have a challenge with the time and you really do. Listen, everybody that's watching or reading the book, you have to make networking your business building time. If you don't spend time building your business, eventually it will die. So, it's a balance, but that is a challenge for most of us. Tell me about a time when networking made a big difference in your business.

Networking has made a huge difference in my business. Why would I say that? Honestly, where I am now has been because of one connection after another. For example, I met my business partner and Toni networking. My business partner and I have the same work ethic and work amazing together. Toni was able to speak into my business life. I am so grateful for you, Toni. I don't just say that. If you don't know her, you need to get to know her. My business went to a different level. I have a different mindset. That doesn't mean I still don't have bumps and bruises. But when I tell you that my mindset to business is definitely because of networking with you and I feel like I can do anything, even if it's a challenge.

Yes, we met at a networking event, and it actually changed the trajectory for both of us. So, as I said, she's my landlord. That means that I'm sitting in the space that we all share and I'm just grateful. Social media is a

form of networking. How has social media helped you to grow your business?

Social media is viral, which is awesome. Because it's viral, I have people who reach out to me even who are not in the same city just because I'm posting what I'm doing, what we have going on in the business, people see it and referrals come from there. So, if Toni Harris Taylor or Marietta are talking about something that we're doing, social media allows others to see and reach out if interested. I will tell anyone, if you're not on social media or you're skeptical about social media, social media is key to allowing you to go viral.

It's an extension of the connection. I tell people all the time that networking and one-to-ones are seed plantings, social media is the fertilizer, or it's the water that helps people to see that you really are who you say you are. One of the businesses we did not mention is that you also have a lounge and an event center – 366 SkyLounge and Event Center. I know that you're growing that by using social media. That's actually one of the things that brought me to you; looking at your talk show on social media. It is a way to be attractive to your ideal client. What mistakes have you seen entrepreneurs make when it comes to networking?

A major mistake is honestly expecting something instead of giving something. You can't walk into a networking event just looking to only gain. What are you looking to give? How are you going to be an answer to someone's problem? How can you be the solution in that room?

Let's elaborate on that a little bit. I need to make some money, otherwise, I'm going to be out of business or

I'm going to have to go get a job. How is it that we think about other people when we are in such need?

What you focus on and pay attention to will grow. Do not focus on your need. Turn the focus to how you can help someone else. You have to know what you have is of value. So walk in the room like you believe that and focus on talking to someone to find out how you can help them. I truly believe, if we help enough people get what they want, ours comes as an automatic.

If more business owners understood that, first of all, the struggle wouldn't be so hard because everybody would be giving all the time and people wouldn't feel alone. It is all about who can serve first. The first one to serve wins. What's your best networking tip?

Just get up and do it. Stop making excuses. The reason why I say that is every major pivotal point in my life and in my business career has been when I've networked. You heard Toni say that I was a former nurse. I got out of nursing because I started networking. Networking led me to saying yes to a networking business. When I started the networking business, I replaced my nursing income doing that business and was able to retire from nursing and I have never looked back. That was one step. Then the next was when my major change happened in this career to do what I'm doing now, it was networking. We have a TV Network and a Lounge and Event Center and more, all because of networking. Just do it.

What does it mean to show up?

Number one, it literally means to show up. You have to be in the room to even receive. You have to be in the room, whether it's virtual or whether it's in person, you have to be in the room. You can't expect anything if you never show up. My second way of showing up is to be present; engaged and present, because if you're in the room and you look totally uninterested and you are not engaged, believe me, no one will want to do business with you.

I hate the chit chat. I hate the schmooze. But it takes that to get to the who are you and what do you do?

People buy you before they buy from you. If we don't talk to people and don't do the small chit chat people will not have the opportunity to get to know you, so they won't buy from you, they won't connect or collaborate with you. Remember they buy ***you*** first.

Describe how your networking has gone viral.

Connection brings connection. Life moves at the speed of relationships. Because of networking with NIA, networking with Toni and Drastic Results, what has happened is my business has gone viral. Toni shares her referral base. She shares and someone else shares; what happens is you go viral. I have people call or ask questions and they don't live here, and that says everything to me. Networking also allowed me to share my book and that went viral. It is just communication. I would honestly say life moves at the speed of relationships.

What's your best strategy for following up?

I don't always do amazing in following up. I take ownership that this is one of my areas of weakness. This is when having a business coach like Toni is vital. I watched you write down everything on a tablet. I wasn't doing that at first. But after you became our coach, I started seeing that and started saying, wait, she puts everything in one tablet, not several tablets. I didn't have an electronic follow up system in place. We're implementing that now because of your coaching. But what I did is simple. I use the tablet system and if I contact anyone, it's written down on the tablet. Then I know I need to contact them again to do a follow up. The tablet system has worked for me. Thank you for that simple tip to help improve what I was not doing very well.

I still love my tablet. There's something about when I write it down. Sometimes I don't even have to go back and look at the list because writing it down solidifies it in my brain. I'm glad to know that a simple, easy, non-electronic tip still works. What's your favorite quote around networking or connecting?

One is "Life moves at the speed of relationships." My favorite quote I love to say all the time is my own quote: "You have greatness within you, Embrace it and let the world see it!"—Sonja Lowe, The Embrace Coach.

You see how she worked that in? That's her quote, by the way. It's not just a quote, it's her quote. What final thoughts can you offer to entrepreneurs who are hesitant to network?

First off, do you really want what's best for you? Do you really want more? If you are satisfied with where you are, then don't network. If you're not satisfied with where you are, my tip is do it. Embrace networking and watch where you go. Your next person may be the very person that refers you to someone who brings you to a whole 'nother level or teaches you something you did not know.

CAITLIN PENNY: BRAND & MARKETING STRATEGIST

CAITLIN PENNY is owner of Copper Theory Creative in Arizona, a full service brand and design agency. The agency is a boutique branding agency in the Chandler-Phoenix area, focusing mainly on branding, design, social media , and web development.

PHONE: 480.738.6377

WEBSITE: CopperTheoryCreative.com

EMAIL: Hello@CopperTheoryCreative.com

For my best friend, Stevie. You've been an inspiration to me since day one. A true CEO in business and in life. You hustle hard, go after your goals, and stand up for what you believe in. You are the woman I've always wanted to be. Love you!

Today's guest is Mrs. Caitlin Penny, who was actually a sponsor at the viral networking conference in 2021. I want to thank her for believing in me and saying yes, and she's chomping at the bit for the next one. So welcome, Caitlin. I appreciate you. Where are you from?

I am from Chandler, Arizona.

Chandler, Arizona, which is a suburb of Phoenix in case you guys don't know. In your own words, Caitlin, who are you and what do you do?

I am Caitlin Penny and I own Copper Theory Creative. We are a boutique branding agency in the Chandler-Phoenix area, and we focus mainly on branding, design, social media now, and web development.

She said social media now, so we'll get into what that means exactly. What got you into your branding business?

I feel like I have that classic story of, I never wanted to work for anybody else. I always wanted to be my own boss. I knew pretty early on and I know that's a rarity in most cases, but by the time I was a junior in high school, I was like, "Graphic design is where it's at. It's happening."

Are you an artist by nature?

I grew up drawing. I wish I had something around here to show you. I'm pretty good at it, if I say so myself. My parents actually were very supportive and sent me to art school after normal school. I've got many, many lessons underneath my belt and I started there. Having artistic talent helped me in the graphic design world.

You are an artistic talent and, like you said, my logo came to you in the middle of the night. I love that.

It did. That notebook on your side table is a key element. I have one for everything, one for middle of the night ideas, one for social media content, and one for sketching.

What made you start networking?

It came pretty naturally to me because I love talking to people, I love hanging out with people, and I love meeting new people. Hearing other entrepreneurship stories was really kind of inspiring to me. I love making a good connection and figuring out how I can help others.

A lot of millennials, and I think you're of that generation, don't love networking. They like being behind the technology for the most part. Right? Honestly, they don't have the people skills. You're a rarity in networking your business. I bet you find that a lot of people are my age when you're out there networking.

I'm usually the youngest person in the room and people are always either turned off or turned on, like there's no middle ground. I took that opportunity to shimmy on in there and talk to people.

Who could be turned off by you? Especially, just because of your age?

Oh yes. I can't tell you how many networking rooms I've been in and they are just like, "Oh, that's nice." Like I'm three years old.

Well, not my people for sure. When it comes to networking, there are many emotions. Some people love it. Others hate it. You've kind of said it, but on the networking meter, have you always been where you loved it, or did you find you had to grow into it?

I definitely grew into it. There's something different about walking into a room with no expectations compared to walking into a room full of your friends. I definitely had the nerves in the beginning, but now I just walk in the room and act like I own it.

Act like you own the room?

It works. Then people want to talk to you. There are many non-verbal queues you can use to make people come to you.

Because it's an attractive posture. I dress up every day for work. You do too. People are often surprised that I show up fully dressed, ready to connect with people. I don't care what you say or how the world has changed, the first impression is still a lasting one.

Even if it's a subconscious-like confidence that you're giving yourself because you got up and got dressed. That's what works for me. I mean, I never sit here and work in my pajamas. Maybe I'll have some comfy pants on, but there's usually some getting ready time.

At least from the waist up, you guys. You and I first met virtually. Because we didn't meet in person untill you came to Houston. I felt like we had known each other forever.

I was like, "This is the first time." You said, "Is it?"

Virtual networking has become more popular since the pandemic. What tips can you share to help someone maximize their virtual networking?

Well, I would definitely show up. Like, put on your face, put on the camera, and just show up. I think that's really the most personal touch you can give virtually. Why are you going to be on Zoom if you can't see somebody's face? Then be present in your mindset too, because if you're just going to show up and let it play in the background, it's not going to do anything for you.

We said it once. We said it twice. We'll probably say it three times before this is over, dress up from the waist up and turn your camera on because it's still about making connections. If you're not present, people can't connect with you.

If you're still somewhere that is mainly virtual then just follow certain protocols and do what you can. You should always have an "it" thing. A hat, a cool background, something to make you stand out from all the other faces in boxes. If I were speaking on Zoom, I would definitely want you to be present. It feels weird when people are sitting there with their cameras off. It feels like no one's paying attention to you. I wouldn't want to do that to you, so don't do it to others.

You said you became an entrepreneur because you never even thought about having a job. But what drives you to stay an entrepreneur? Because this game is not easy.

There is no plan B. I'm just going to throw that out there. That's my kind of my motivation every day. I mean, it's as simple as that for me and it works. I can't imagine myself being happier, working for someone else than I am right now.

Okay on the not wanting to work for someone else, and being your own boss. I agree with you.

Well, I want to work my dream. I mean, I love to help other people, but I'd rather work towards mine than be a minion working for someone else's dream.

Tell me about a time you didn't want to show up, you pushed ahead and you're glad you did.

Well, a few months back, I officially got a logo on the side of a building. I have like five of them now.

Describe what that means. A logo on side the side of a building.

Like on the side of a building, like on the building.

On the side of a building? Outside? Like on the marquee?

Yep! It was super exciting. I've had a few before that and I always go to visit. This time they invited me to their open house, and I felt a little bit uncomfortable because they're lawyers. It was a little bit out of my realm. I was like, "Ah, I don't know." It came back to that "I don't know anybody in the room" thing. But then I went and walked around and introduced myself. It was a small setting as well. It was more intimidating to me in that sense, as opposed to a whole room of people. Nervously, I just shook everyone's hand and introduced myself. I met people from the chambers out here. I made many connections. They keep sending me people since I showed up that day and since I finished their logo. It doesn't come so much from, "Hey, do you know this person?" Someone asked them and then it's like two references away, if that makes sense. It's two off of the main person that I worked for. I keep getting phone calls and referrals from them. I am glad I did that because they're such fun women.

That means you do amazing work, but let's go back to the question. You showed up when you didn't feel like it. You were out of your comfort zone, but look how it has snowballed from there. The tea in the message is, to go viral, you must show up even when you don't feel like it. Even when it's out of your comfort zone. Congratulations for having five logos on a marquee. That was one time, but tell me about a time where networking made a big difference in your business.

I'm thinking about this conference that I sponsored in November, the Viral Networking Conference. I don't know if I've even updated you, but I've made a lot off of it. I was nervous. I mean, it was across states. I had never spoken in front of a crowd that big. I was freaking out all over the place. Mr. Glenn Walker had to give me a pep talk in the hallway right before I went on stage. Thank you for that Glenn. I can't even explain it. Your people, I know, are great and you create such a great community. Being in Arizona and watching you from afar definitely had an impact. Then showing up in the room, it was like a whole new world. The audience was welcoming and giving, and everyone was happy, positive, and supportive. When I got up there, I think I did a catwalk down the hallway. It was great!

You were celebritized at my event. Two years in a row you had the most appointments. Because I demand appointments. You must schedule one-to-ones when you come to my events. Two years in a row, you had them. Honestly, I think the time you showed up and it made a big difference was the first event. You learned how to do one-to-ones -- the art of doing them. You scheduled the most, and I know you benefited, made money from that event as an attendee. Then you took the drastic step to be a sponsor and that turned into gold for you. I can't wait for you to sponsor again this year.

Thank you. It's official!

I guess it is. I just said it on the recording. Well, why would I not bring you back? Everybody loves you. You do amazing work. You honor your commitments.

Thank you. I think the journey has been great too. Because that first event was, what, three years ago or something like that? It feels like so far away. That's right. Pandemic time. But when you give people a formula to do that, it was easy. Then naturally I'm competitive. I was like, "Challenge accepted."

You are competitive. You mentioned social media. Social media is a form of networking. How has social media helped you grow your business?

I mean, it's so important nowadays. I compare it to 2005 when people were like, "You don't have a website?" That's pretty much social media now. If you don't have it, as unprofessional as social media is, people don't think it's professional if you don't have it. It's starting to catch on and now platforms like LinkedIn are business focused. It's not so much of that scroll through mindless nonsense that you usually deal with on social media. When you utilize the right platforms to promote your business specifically, it's like a whole different algorithm to figure out what works for your business and what is the best response. I've recently been doing the Facebook Lives with Ronda and Dai and people love me on video. I hated doing it at first. I said, "Okay, fine." Then I started being consistent, which helped my presence and personality comes through. When you're authentic in your business, people like it and people watch out for it. I've literally shown up to a networking event and people were from across the room, "Oh my god, I know your face from LinkedIn. I like your videos." That's how we make connections now.

I love that you have embraced video. That came out of showing up and coming to the community and having peers. We have a lot of positive peer pressure in the

Drastic Results community and the Network In Action community. We have a lot of positive peer pressure that get you out of your comfort zone. Your videos have been excellent. You mentioned adding a social media piece to your business. Tell me more.

I guess the keywords here are collaborative partners, your power partners. Joint ventures. That sounds good. Over the past year, I have started creating those joint ventures. One of them is with a social media strategist. Most of the time, how my business is set up, it's kind of a walk-through, a one-stop shop. After branding, after graphic design, after all that stuff, people ask, "Well, what about social media?" For a while I said, "Oh, okay. I'll design the graphics." Well, in case you didn't know, you can't post a graphic without some sort of content, and I wasn't writing the content. I had to fill that void. Our social media strategist, Megan, is an expert at all of this and she focuses on the strategy per each platform. Now we sell packages like that together. I get to do my part where I'm an expert at and she gets to do her part. I actually met her at Kim O'Bannon's NIA meeting.

Network In Action is in action again. I love that. What mistakes have you seen other people make when it comes to networking?

Oh, standing in the corner not talking to anyone. Why'd you even come? I mean, I get the nervousness. But now, I walk right up to you. I ask, "Hey, what are you doing?"

People nurse a drink at the bar. They don't talk to anyone. That's talking to our introvert friend, right? They're an introvert and they don't know what to say or do. What tips would you give them beyond the showing up?

I don't only show up. Like physically I'm there, but I don't walk in the room without a plan. Let's put it that way. But I also don't go in with a bunch of expectations. I plan to make valuable connections with people. That doesn't matter if it's three or if it's six, but I do get people to get on my calendar while I'm standing there. Then I listen to what these people have to say. Usually it's something like, "Hey, how's it going? My name's Caitlin. I'm blah, blah, blah, blah, blah." It can be robotic sometimes. I actually listen to the story being told, or I try to ask a different question other than "Who are you and what do you do? That way there's a personal connection there. That's my favorite part.

A personal connection. You've given a lot of gold there, but I'm going to ask specifically what is your best networking tip?

I would say, be present, be there. If you're going to be there, put in the effort. You're there. You did it. You're already halfway done. Just do the thing. You came for a reason.

That goes into the next question. What does it mean to show up? Be present. Here's the other thing. I know you believe in this, you also have to be willing to help other people.

Yes. I usually ask at the end of any kind of networking meeting or discovery call or in person, what I can do for you? It's not, "What service can I sell you?" It's "Who would you like to meet? What are you looking for? What is your next business goal? How can I help? Maybe I know someone that's a CPA." It doesn't have to be sales all the time.

This is where most networking falls short. What is your best advice for following up?

My best strategy for following up is a three point contact system. I will email you once after we connect. I usually ask when to follow up with you. I will check in with you on that day. If I don't hear from you, I will again, send you another email or a note probably about at the two week mark. I will check in again with the same sort of message, "Hey, how's it going? Just wanted to check in on this project you wanted to work on. Would you still like to work together?" Then there is a final third time that I will check in if I have not heard from you. I just say, "Hey, I know that you probably are busy being an entrepreneur, but I wanted to check in and see if you still wanted to work on this project. No worries either way, just let me know." The second way I follow up with my clients is to send them postcards. I have designed my own postcards and it just says, "Thanks for working with me." You get it in the mail, snail mail. I write a personal note on there and it just says thanks. It has a little picture or avatar of me and that's pretty much it. Usually people call me and say, "Hey, I got your cute card in the mail."

Describe how your networking has gone viral.

I think that my networking has gone viral in a few different ways. One, social media. I am consistent on social media and I invite people to follow me on social media when I'm networking. That means that I get more connections, more follows, and then I get more engagement on my online platforms. Right now, it's a great way to view my art, view the work, and view the clients I've worked with. That way you get an idea of who I am and what kind of people I help. The other way my networking has gone viral is I started speaking. Last year, I sponsored Toni's event and that was one of the first times I've spoken in front of that many people. I was nervous because I'm not a public speaker, but I made it one of my goals to get more speaking gigs. That helps me connect with my audience. I think I have a good stage presence and I'm usually interactive, happy, and bubbly when I'm in a room. That attracts a lot of people and it makes them feel comfortable walking up to me and saying hello. That part is super important to me because I love making those connections. Being your authentic self in your business, is a great representation of who you are and it attracts your right customers.

What is your favorite quote about networking or connecting?

I have been obsessed with Daymond John recently. If you know me, you know I love me some Shark Tank. I saw one of his videos recently and he said, "Don't wait for the perfect time, you'll wait forever. Always take advantage of the time you're given." So awesome. That applies to everything in my life. I am trying to now use that quote in my more personal pieces of life because I definitely do it in business and it works and it pays off.

What final thoughts can you offer to entrepreneurs who are hesitant to network?

I think the biggest final thought I can give you is to be yourself. When you're real, when you're genuine, when you're authentic, people can see that and it gives them something to connect with. It gives them something to relate to you with.

DR. SONJA OGLETREE SATANI: BUSINESS COACH

DR. SONJA OGLETREE SATANI
Air Force Veteran, Professor, Speaker, Consultant, Business Expert & Strategist. Dr. Sonja Ogletree Satani equips audiences with the skills to conquer any challenge and face their fears head on whether it is personal, or business related. Dr. Sonja Ogletree Satani was featured in *Forbes* magazine as seen in the June 16, 2014, issue spotlighting Southeast Women Business Leaders and the award-winning *Women In Business* magazine of the American Business Women's Association.

PHONE: 843.920.3222.

WEBSITE: CorporateCycleConsulting.com

EMAIL: Sonja@CorporateCycleConsulting.com

I dedicate this to my family, aspiring business owners, and entrepreneurs.

I am here with my friend, colleague, mini me. I got a lot of mini me's running around here, Dr. Sonja Ogletree Satani, from Dayton, Ohio and now lives in Charleston, South Carolina. Welcome. Tell us who you are and what you do.

I am Dr. Sonja Ogletree Satani. I am the owner and business coach with Corporate Cycle Consulting and a Franchise Owner with Network in Action – Corporate Cycle Connections. I specialize in business growth and development and help entrepreneurs get certified so they can IGNITE their profits.

Awesome. You specialize in helping those businesses to get prepared to go after government and corporate contracts, right? Why did you decide to get in NIA?

I attended your Viral Networking event, and I was able to meet some of your colleagues that are already affiliated with NIA, and I just loved it. Well, at first, I thought we did not have one here in Charleston, but it turned out that we did, but I never heard of it. Initially my thought was, this will be a fantastic opportunity to bring this type of networking opportunity to Charleston, and especially to bring to business owners that are looking to grow and to expand their operations. So, from a networking standpoint, it is especially important to have those connections, to make those connections, especially for those businesses that are just starting out because a lot of times they don't know who to connect to. So, for me to take advantage of this opportunity, I wanted to be able to help these business owners. I am sure you are familiar with the proverb or the saying, right? "You give a man a fish, they eat for a day. You teach them how to fish; they'll be able to eat for a lifetime." But now being able to connect the networking side, you can show them where to fish and introduce them to the other fisher men or the other fish in the pond, if you will.

One of the things that I love too is Network in Action, even though they are local to your group, there is a national presence, as well, for those business owners who want to meet people and connect people nationally. We are like family. I am so excited for you and congratulations

on taking that drastic step. So how did Corporate Cycle Consulting come about?

Corporate Cycle Consulting came about for several reasons. Number one, I am a project manager behind the scenes. Serving as a program project manager, lean six sigma black belt, you know businesses go through different cycles from the startup to becoming a small, to medium, to large size, but there are a lot of challenges that go through each of those phases. For me, it just made sense to help these businesses to navigate through these phases and to be able to provide the roadmap for each stage that they are going through.

Now you have a compelling story about why you left corporate and started your own business. Do you want to share that a little bit?

I had been training my replacement in preparation for a promotion that HR told me I was going to receive. I knew this position was mine because I had checked off all the boxes for the requirements and then some. I walked into the office with my power suit on, my hair, nails and makeup were done because today was the day for the announcement. As I entered the building my colleagues was congratulating me and telling me how excited they were for me to be in this new position as the Vice President for my division. I sat down at my desk with my head swollen like a helium balloon and I opened my email. I could not believe what I saw. The position I was so ready to have, was given to the person I hired and trained. I was pissed! How dare they?! I sat there fuming. I remembered what Madam CJ Walker said, "you can't sit down and wait for opportunities to come, you have to get up and make them." So, I got up and started packing my stuff. I turned in my keys, my computer, my badge and left a well-paying job. As I was driving home, I thought to myself, *what am I going to do now?* What was my husband going to say? I knew it was time to invest in me, it was time to build an opportunity in which I was the leader of my own destiny. My vision was so clear about what I wanted for my consulting business – Corporate Cycle Consulting.

I struggled with marketing my business and telling people about my new business. I found myself as a generalist trying to help everyone and yet I was getting no one. My personal funds started getting low trying to sustain this new business. I was feeling overwhelmed, scared, and I needed help; so, I got a business coach. I build a tribe to give me the support I needed. In my search for support, resources, and a way to build a 7-figure business. I found a proven method that guarantees any business owner to make money in 90 days or less. I used the solution for myself so that I can clarify my vision, create an action plan, and commit to adding new clients as well as strengthen my confidence as a business owner and leader. Now, I can help aspiring business owners who were just like me struggling to get their ideas and business off the ground. I was looking for training, consulting, and business connections.

Now as a business coach, I can give business owners a roadmap to help them start and grow a successful business and generate a minimum of $10K monthly through our consulting and training programs as well as help entrepreneurs make meaningful connections with my networking group. I used the solution for others, and I have successfully trained over 1000 business owners and entrepreneurs since I launched Corporate Cycle Consulting in 2012 and in January 2022, I bought a franchise-Network in Action, Corporate Cycle Connections which adds to my brand and now I am able to provide a way for my clients to get consulting, training, coaching, and connections and increase their ROI by 76%. I am excited to be able to help my business owners get more clients, establish connections, and teach them how to grow their business and make more money.

Think back to that time, or even earlier, what made you know that you had to start networking to find your relationships and customers and all of that? What was that turning point?

I will share with you that I had gone to different organizations and social events. I would introduce myself and explain what my business was, and because they did not know who I was, it was harder for me to get those connections, to get my foot in the door. But the more that they saw me, the more that they took the time to get to know me, it became a easier because now they trust me. Now these are the individuals that are coming to me for guidance and for help. But it was not easy at first. I was networking with the wrong people. So that put a strain in really exposing and growing my business and taking it to the level that I needed. It took a while to get there; but I will tell you, I am super excited that I did not stop. I did not give up. I was able to connect with the right people to really help launch and grow my own business.

When it comes to networking, emotionally, people fall all over the place. They love it. They hate it. Rarely are people in the middle. It is okay. Usually, they have strong emotions. Now you just bought a networking

organization, so I know you are on the love spectrum. Why do you love networking?

I just love helping people. I love giving back. For me, it has never been about me. It is about how I can help that other person achieve what it is that they are looking for. When you help enough people get what they want, you are able to get what you want. But in getting what you want, you must know what you want. When they are asking, "Hey, what do you need?" For me, I am so quick to say, "I'm good," because I am that giver. But one of the things that I have learned as a business owner, is that you have to be specific in the ask, or otherwise you're going to get whatever you get and how you get it, or you might not get anything at all.

Now you are going to be teaching your Network in Action members how to strategically network so that they fall in love with it as well. So, since the pandemic, which does not look like it is going to go away, virtual networking has become more popular. How do you feel about virtual networking?

It definitely saves money on gas, food, and hotel. Virtual networking provides opportunities to share your business and for you to be on various platforms, whether you are on Zoom or WebEx or Microsoft Meeting Teams, this gives you an opportunity to meet with people across the nation. You get to meet with people who typically say, "Oh, I don't have time." Because pre-pandemic, we were traveling to go from meeting to meeting. Now, you have more flexibility and can save that drive time to fill it with new conversations. With virtual meetings, it is easier to get on the schedule. You are saving some time to get from one location to another, missing opportunities, but also having information right there. So, sometimes if you are afraid to share your market dominating position, or what your business pitch is, you can pull it up on your computer. Nobody will know that you are reading because you are looking into the camera. Of course, as there are things that you want to share, you can put together a little cheat sheet. I want to make sure that when I am making a connection with someone, not only am I asking what they do and what kind of people they like to associate with, or what the best referral that I can give. But all of that is right there, at your fingertips. You do not have to scramble. No one knows that you put together your own personal virtual business meeting checklist.

Entrepreneurship is not easy. What is the driving force behind you staying an entrepreneur?

You know for me, I am an overachiever, as many people have called me. It starts with the mindset and what you want to achieve for yourself. People have different motivations. I have always put everyone else first. As an entrepreneur, I wanted to build and create a business, I wanted something that was mine. I wanted to be able to create a legacy, to leave a legacy; not only for my family, but also for my community and who I touch. So not just on a local level, but on a global scale. I have had the honor and pleasure of meeting people from around the world. From previous travels of serving in the military, or even serving as an ambassador for my college, or even being part of the United Nations. For me, it goes back to Oprah Winfrey; where everyone has a story, and there is something to be learned from every experience. Not only am I learning from others, but I am also able to share my experience as well and being able to launch Corporate Cycle Consulting. Of course, with NIA, Corporate Cycle Connections, we can learn from each other and to help each other grow.

Well, you are an inspiration to me. I just need you to not put on any more hats, lady. Tell me about a time that you did not want to show up. "I'm tired. I don't want to go." But you pushed ahead, and you are glad you did.

I tell you from being a mom, a wife, a professor, a business owner and coach, people are counting on you. So, no matter how tired, how sick you might feel, you get your hot toddy, get your body right. So that way, the next day you can push forward and to move forward. For me, I know that people are counting on me, and I do not want to let them down. I have already let myself down, but I do not want to continue to let myself down. That goes back to my overachiever-ism, and my husband tells me, "You always want to be in the forefront, in the limelight." Well, that is his perception, but I do not see it as being in the limelight. I see it as being there, being that loyal person to help that individual move forward. You must set the example for others to follow, especially as a leader in the community.

Everybody has some challenges with their networking. Tell me what is your challenge with networking?

Sometimes I find myself being the worker bee if you will. So, there are times when I know that I should be making those connections or putting myself out in the forefront. If there are people that need something, I will connect them. I do not always focus on what I need, so that has been a challenge. I just put everybody first.

Tell me about a time when networking made a dramatic difference in your business.

I will share with you. When I launched Corporate Cycle Consulting, I became a member of the American Business Women's Association. That gave me the initial platform to really launch and to become a speaker and to share with these women how to start and grow their own business. Because of that networking opportunity, and because of the leadership opportunities they were able to see within me, within the first two years of being in that organization, not only did I start off within the first 30 days of serving as the co-chair for membership in my local chapter; but then the next year I became the secretary on the executive board. That very next year, I became the chapter president, and then shortly after that, I ran for district vice president within the organization. Now, even though I did not win the first time, that exposure to that network, that exposure to women that served as my mentors, encouraged me. "Don't give up, come back again." Well, I was not planning to give up. So, I did go back the very next year. I ran again for district vice president and won and was a 2016 Top 10 Business Woman. Then the very next year ran for national secretary-treasurer and won. Then in 2017 became the National President for the American Business Woman's Association. Because of this volunteered experience of serving and leading, of growing and learning has encouraged me not to give up. It has helped me to strengthen my confidence, improve my business acumen and skill, and become a better leader. Because of utilizing the networking opportunities, it has taken me all over the US, and Puerto Rico, I have been able to meet women that are business owners. I have been able to grow and expand my network and build personal and genuine relationships that have lasted a lifetime.

Social media is a form of networking. So, tell me where social media has made a difference in your business? Which, by the way, is what kept us connected. How did we get back to this?

Social media, on a personal level, has allowed me to connect with a lot of business owners, friends, and relatives. But I tell you, and I will be honest, I still struggle with social media, because on the outside, I am very extroverted, but when it comes to the privacies and what I am doing, I'm very introverted on the social media side. So, for me, especially as a business owner, it is a big push to really put the company out there, and to make sure that it is there. But also, the challenge that I have is just finding the time. I know you can schedule, you can plan what you want to post, but I would rather do the connecting side than the social media side, because there is still that disconnect, if you will. I would rather touch and call you than send a message or a post.

What mistakes have you seen other entrepreneurs make when it comes to networking?

The biggest mistake is the follow up or not following up. Another mistake is "Here's my business card. Call me." You know what happens with those business cards, right? They get stuck in our pockets. You open your purse, and you are like, "Oh, who is that person again? How did I meet them?" You just forget, and you lose touch. So, it is always important, and Toni, you drive this all the time, and I am also a huge believer of it, is when you make that connection, schedule the appointment right away. Book that time, that one on one, whatever you are going to do, just get it done. Why wait? Even, for me, with balancing business, family, volunteering, and other tasks—people are saying "Sonja, you're so busy. How do you do that? How do you get that done, that job done so fast?" Because I do not wait. So, if it is something intentional that you are trying to do, that you are trying to change, you have got to be ready and willing to just get it done. Like Nike, just do it. If you stay ready, you will be ready. If you are getting ready, you may miss your opportunity because you are not ready. You just have to do it!

What does it mean to you, when I say show up, you know that is my saying, what does it mean to you to show up?

Showing up does a lot. Number one, it gives you access to the information. Number two, in getting the access, you can ask questions to the people or presenter in the room. Number three, when you show up, it gives you an opportunity to practice new skills sets until you're able to master and do it for what you need, but if you're not there, how would you even know what to do, when to do it, how to do it, all that great stuff.

But it also gives you an opportunity to connect with those from which you are learning. They get to see you as well. Then, finally, part of showing up, as Toni says, you show up, you blow up, you go up and it does not matter the organizations that you are with. Even if you are still in corporate and you have not transitioned to becoming that business owner, you still must show up to the meeting. How are you going to know what is going on? Or what is your role and responsibility if you are not there. So, whether it is a need-to-know basis, or even if you are serving as the recording secretary for your organization or group; so even though you are there, you might not be the decision maker, but because you are there, you're in the know. So, showing up allows you to be knowledgeable.

Do you have any other tips about following up?

Yes. My tip is do not wait for someone else to follow up because a lot of times it is like, "Oh yeah, we'll get in contact." You are waiting for the other person to contact you. Take the initiative, just take the initiative.

Describe how your networking has gone viral.

I am still working and developing new and creative ways to take my networking to the next level and making it go viral. But I will tell you, having the opportunity to meet people from all over the world, such as Russia, from India, from Japan, from Spain, has been amazing. Sometimes it is not all about the transaction, but it is about the relationship. People must understand that when you are networking, you are building relationships and you are not building transactions. The transactions come as a result of the relationships that you build.

What is your favorite quote around networking or connecting?

My favorite networking quote is by Oprah Winfrey who said, "You have to surround yourself with people who are going to lift you higher." So, I have been intentional on selecting core professionals and friends who have my best interest in mind. These individuals encourage me and serve as my sounding board, my prayer warriors, and are there to keep me and my business lifted. They are not jealous individuals or backstabbers. It is important for business owners and entrepreneurs to understand and know who is in their group that is going to lift them higher.

DAI SMITH: PRODUCTIVITY ORGANIZING COACH

DAI SMITH is the owner and founder of Simplicity By Day, LLC, the organizing & productivity consulting company that provides simple and organized solutions for entrepreneurs, professionals and parents alike. She is a certified professional organizer and has undergrad and graduate business degrees and is a design school graduate. She is an award- winning sales/ marketing professional who specializes in productivity and décor organizing and is a member of National Association of Productivity and Organizing.

PHONE: 281.609.9986
WEBSITE: SimplicityByDay.com
EMAIL: SimplicityByDay@gmail.com

To the woman who personifies purpose, passion, and poise and who's shoulders I stand on, my grandmother, Jearldean Isom.

Today's guest is one of my favorite clients, Dai Smith of Simplicity By Day. Tell everybody who you are and what do you do.

I am Dai Smith, the productivity consultant and digital organizer. I help small business owners to streamline their systems so they can be more present, more productive, and more profitable.

How did the idea for your business come about?

I started my business as a professional organizer, organizing pantries and homes. After coaching with Toni, I discovered my true passion and true value to my clients comes in the form of digital organizing and productivity consulting. I found a way to leverage my professional organizing skills and processes to those who needed help with their digital assets and technology, and the systems that were giving them a headache and making them feel all over the place. I was able to bring order and help them get organized and found that niche of who I wanted to serve.

As a busy business owner with systems all over the place, you helped me too through your VIP Day and helped me to streamline my systems. We are both working together to help each other with our systems. What made you start networking?

I have always been an extrovert. I like meeting new people and learning about their lives and all that good stuff, but I felt like I wasn't meeting the right people in my business. I always saw networking as more of a social thing. I never really made the connection for business and intentional strategic conversations. When I heard Toni speak about sales and marketing through networking, a light bulb went off for me, and I thought, "Well, perhaps this is how I can get in front of the people that I need to get in front of." Networking then became like a business necessity and more intentional for me because I realized that's how I get in front of people. When you build those connections and you find common ground and how you can partner with people, that's really the essence of networking. That is how I really started networking more.

When it comes to networking, people either love it or hate it, and you've already said you're an extrovert. Does that mean that all extroverts love networking? Where are you on the scale?

I was on the scale of, I like meeting new people, but I felt like networking came across kind of pushy. Like I have to go. I want to sell you something. It didn't make me feel comfortable wanting to network as a business owner because I felt like I would be pushing my services on others.

That's what I thought maybe a couple of years ago, but now I see networking as just connecting with people. You go in and you understand that you're learning about someone, and it can be social, but you guys are in a partnership to help one another out. That makes networking look and feel differently now. It doesn't feel cheesy or fake or disingenuous; well, that's the way I approach it anyways. I'm going to learn from you. I'm going to help you. How can we help each other? It feels like I'm building another community of people that I hadn't had in my life before through my business.

Virtual networking has become more popular since the pandemic. What tips can you share to maximize virtual networking?

I feel like whatever I'm going to say, if you all follow Toni, you probably have already heard this, but it works. Always have your bio and your links ready to go, make sure that you have the https:// ready in front of your website, so that it's a hot link as Toni say. When they click on it in the chat box, it takes them to the page, just creating a bio of who you are, your tagline, how they can get in touch with you.

Don't make it too long. Have that ready to go, because most virtual networking asks people to introduce themselves. Or if you're going to be chatting one off, you can pop that in there, have that ready to go. That's one tip. Then another tip is, I know since being virtual, most of us want to do multiple things at once. You want to minimize the screen and go check your email and it's hard not to, I struggle. I think that if you could just bring it back and just really try to focus in, give that person your undivided attention, whoever's speaking, because they prepared this for you. You may learn a thing or two. Really try to just stay tuned in to the virtual platform. That would be my two things.

I love that. I struggle with that too. I love virtual networking, but staying connected, staying focused, closing other tabs, silencing the cell phone. All those things are great tips to maximize your virtual networking and listening. It's temporary. It lasts for one hour in most cases. Like you said, the speaker (and we are both speakers) appreciate having engagement and people paying attention so that we aren't distracted. Then yes, that's how you and I met, right?

So, you're a corpopreneur. One of my other coaching clients came up with that corpopreneur, which means you are a corporate boss literally. You are a corporate boss, plus you have your own business. Your corporate job is nothing to sneeze at. I mean, entrepreneurship is hard. Why did you have to pursue becoming an entrepreneur?

That's a question I ask myself often, but I've always wanted to be an employer. I've always wanted to create something, to give people opportunities for jobs, to build a life. That's the core of why I'm doing what I'm doing. But whenever

I say I'm going to do something, I do it. I go all in. When I said, I'm going to start this business, I meant it. I started two and a half years ago. I'm all in, no matter if I still have a job, no matter that I'm raising little kids, I'm just going to go for it. I'm glad that I have, because I feel like I've been able to reach people in a way I wouldn't have. If I was just working on my corporate job and influencing people in my circles that I didn't even know I was influencing. In 2020 when Kobe Bryant passed away, I remember one of the things that he said, "Well, we talked about the Mamba mentality and how you never know when your last day is, you just have to go for it and give it a 100%." That really motivated me, because I was tethering the line like, "I'm going to do this. I'm going to work. I'm going to do that." But that gave me permission to say, "You know what, I'm going to try and I'm going to do it. I'm going to give it my all, no matter what." That's been driving me when it gets challenging when I'm running around, crazy balancing everything. I remember that. I remember that I have people watching me and I have shoulders that I'm standing on and I have goals that I want to achieve. So, I'm going to keep going.

I love all my clients. I'm like the mama, I love all my kids, but there's certain kids that do exactly what mama says do and there's a little extra fondness with them and that's you. You will try anything that I tell you to do. If you like, "Okay?" Yeah. You say it and you try it. Then, "Oh, my gosh, Toni, this is what happened." I'm so proud that you got one of your top highest paid clients through networking. Do you want to tell that story?

Toni connected me with the group and I spoke for them and I just clicked with the program director and networked with her, stayed in touch with her and our businesses complimented each other. So, really we were again networking to support one another. She found an opportunity to refer me to her client. So that immediately connected the trust factor because now her client is like, "Oh, you want me to go today for organizing?" She came straight to me, with a wonderful client. I was in the process of raising my rates and fine tuning my value. I was able to do that. This client was on board. I started the year off with my highest paying client in my entire business history, not to mention I was already booked and busy with other clients that have come from Toni, and networking, but that was just a cherry on top.

I just love hearing that story because it took six months, eight months for something to come out of that relationship. Not that you were intending for something... but it takes time you, guys. It is not immediate gratification with networking, but when there's a real connection, people find a way to refer you. They find a way to collaborate with you, and that's the beauty of networking. So, tell me, Dai, about a time that you didn't want to show up. You pushed ahead and you're glad you did.

I wasn't going to join. Let's see, one of the networks across the nations, they come every month and I'm thinking I'll catch the next one. I think it was two months or two visits ago and I got on that call and I was using my methods with Toni, popping in the chat. I was engaged. I remember I had hit a lull in my one to ones. Honestly, I was trying to catch up and I got on there and it reignited my one-to-one. I remember I was getting my acuity schedule for how many visits I had for the week. It was one week. Then after that NIA Network With the Nation, it was 7 or 8 that week. I had all these appointments throughout the week and I'm filling them in and so much has come that I've joined another networking group. I've brought on some partners through that. Just being exposed to people in the right market where I want to be. All these coaches and consultants I partnered with and got on some podcasts because of that. I mean, there was such a wealth of people on that call and I'm so glad I got on because I was just like, "I'm going to catch the next one. I hadn't been on in a while." Everyone on that call said that they had a great turnaround from just engaging with people. So, you just never know who you're going to meet.

You never know who you're going to meet. For those of you watching Network with the Nations as part of NIAs events, and we bring in all NIA members across the country, they are invited to come to a zoom call where they go into breakouts and it's fast paced, but you meet some incredible people. NIA is not the cheapest networking and we make no apologies for that. But the people that are there are serious, because they're invested. I'm glad to hear that. That's a great story. So tell me, what are some of your challenges with networking?

Because I'm a "corpreneur" and a mom of young kids, and I know everyone is busy, but I feel like I always struggling to find time to network. I feel like I was being pulled in many directions when I signed up to the network and I'm preparing here and taking time away from something else. That is for sure my biggest challenge with networking. It's balancing how many events I go to, how many virtual events I'm on. That is a challenge, but what I've done, because I'm solution oriented in 2022, I commit, I set boundaries. I commit to a couple nights a week that I'm going to network, one can be virtual and one could be in person.

But what that does for me is it makes me value which ones I choose. If I'm going to be there, I'm going to be there. I'm going to show up, I'm going to be present. I'm going to make the most of it. I'm going to connect with people in the chat. I'm about to go all in because I know that I only have two a week, so I got to make most of it.

You've given me some great success stories, but tell me about a time when networking made a big difference in your business. It might be that time with Christian, I'm not sure.

I mean, that was definitely a big success, but I will speak more holistically. I remember in our Viral Networking Conference, I was a sponsor and you had me create a mind map and my mind map, it starts here, Dai-Toni, and then it stems out with all these circles. I was just, she asked me to create it and here I am writing it out.

I didn't even realize how many circles and lines came from that one circle of Toni and I, and I feel like I'm a pretty social person. I got a lot of friends and stuff and associates, but man, what the networking stuff of my business and how it blossomed. I mean that mind map had 10, 12 lines. That was just in October... this has grown even more, I don't even think it's the same between me mapping it and presenting it...it had already grown in the month. Now between November and now that probably has doubled. So to me, it's just a testament of networking and being connected to the right people, because of course, you could be connected to people and they could burn you and you are like, "I don't want to be involved there," but that's not the case with Toni. That's not the case with most of the people, anyone really, that she's connected with realtors, crowd, coaching, different associations. I've just been running in circles with good people, good business owners that I've learned a lot from. It solidified me as a business owner. This is an asset that I have now as a business owner. I have all these connections. If any of my clients need anything, I can find it for them, from people that I know and trust, many of my family members need anything it's right here. This is another asset that I have for my business, the fact that I am so well connected in this space internationally, nationally in Houston, you name it.

My girl helped me to get organized. Let's talk about social media. Social media is a form of networking. How has social media helped you to grow your business?

Well, I'm a millennial, so I'm a huge fan of social media. It's a hobby of mine. When I started my business, I thought that was the perfect avenue to socialize myself as a business owner. I feel like I have initially chosen the social platforms that I'm comfortable with, the Facebook and Instagram, because that's what I'm on. But what I've realized is that there are other platforms that fit more in my target market, like LinkedIn, the YouTube. Even Pinterest, if that's what I'm focusing on. With social media, really, you have to look at it as what's going to get you in front of your target market and create a strategy to where you're messaging the right way. You have everything in place so that when you do meet that person they know exactly what you're doing and who you are and what you're offering. So being a business owner has made social media more strategic for sure versus social. I have used it to leverage brand awareness. I socialize that I'm just not, Dai Smith, this and that. I'm actually a productivity expert. I'm able to make that connection across all platforms, or at least I try to.

We have not mentioned that you're the author of two books.

My book sales came from social media and promoting everything came from really social media. But yeah, social media definitely has helped me with that as well.

What mistakes have you seen entrepreneurs make when it comes to networking and what's your best networking tip?

Mistakes, not doing it, being afraid to do it. Whether it is doubting yourself or just thinking that it's not important. That's the biggest mistake, not doing and not showing up. So, the tip would be to just show up, just put yourself together virtually or in person. Bring a friend, if you need to, if you don't feel comfortable going by yourself, just bring a friend. But the mistake would be not doing it. The tip would be to push yourself to do it. If you expect different things, you have to do things differently.

I love the bring a friend tip right now. Don't bring an introvert friend like you, right? Bring that extrovert friend who's going to push you out of your comfort zone. Do you remember the time that five or six of us went to one event and we started by saying, "Who do you want to meet? Who do you want to meet? Who do you want to meet?" And we started networking for each other. Then it became about searching the room. It was a large room. Who can we introduce each other to? Wasn't that fun?

I got a client out of that. I got a speaking opportunity, another partner, and a client. It came from that.

Take a friend with you. In your mind you just said your tip is to go, but what does it mean to show up?

To show up to me means being present, not being distracted and maybe being willing to learn something, be open minded because you're not there to sell, but just show up to learn and just be able to have someone pouring into you.

Absolutely, and an additional tip for the audience is, besides turning the camera on, I just cannot believe how many people still come to events and don't turn the camera on. Always raise your hand. Always make a comment, ask a question, say who you are. The other tip is to be branded. You see how Dai is branded? She doesn't have her junky room; which she don't have junky rooms, because she's an organizer but people have their whole junky room in the background. It's like 'clean that mess up'.

People like me are looking, and I may just find your cat. I have kids wandering, so I can't talk about nobody. Right?

What is your best strategy for following up?

I use my iPad. I'm a digital organizer. Every time I'm on a call, I make a note for the event. I have an AI file and I just jot down people's names and asterisk them. That's something that I do when I want to follow up. But another easy way is while you're in the meeting send a private chat and send an appointment. That way they're on your calendar. There's no need to follow up. That appointment is set or they've gotten on your calendar. If you're like me, you got all their information, you got their email, you got everything, so that appointment is set. But if you don't do that and you save the chat, what you can do is set a reminder for yourself. Every Thursday I go through my administrative task and I go through an email or go through a followup on the weekly event. Set a system to follow up. Don't just have the chat sitting there, saying you don't follow up. That's what I would say to do.

You've already described it. The question is, describe how your networking has gone viral. Is there anything more you want to add to that?

To go viral means that people are talking about you in a room that you are not in. I thought about that, going viral to me is having people be advocates for you, right? They've witnessed what you do. They've witnessed your skillset or your personality or the value you bring. Now they're spreading the word for you. They're being salespeople for you. That's what I've experienced through networking because that's where referrals come from. That's how I've gotten clients. I'm not in that meeting. I'm not in that room. I'm not in that chat, but someone can connect me to them.

What's your favorite quote around networking or connecting?

One of my all-time favorite authors, speakers, activists, women in general, a drastic woman, a survivor, Maya Angelou, said, "People may not remember what you said, people may not remember what you do, but they always remember how you made them feel." I am always trying to leave people better for having met me or talked with me more than when I leave, than when I met them. When I'm connecting with people or when I'm networking with them, I want them to feel differently. I want them to either feel like I can help me, or they can do this. Or if I'm doing it, they can do it.

TONI HARRIS TAYLOR: MARKETING COACH & COMMUNITY BUILDER

TONI HARRIS TAYLOR is a marketing/sales coach and an international speaker. She is known as The Networking Queen and The Coach that Connects™. Drastic Results Marketing and Sales Coaching helps entrepreneurs get known, get connected, and get paid! She teaches the how-to of leveraging branding, networking, and speaking to attract clients magnetically to grow to six figures and beyond. She also has a videocast where she interviews successful entrepreneurs to touch, move and inspire the audience to stay in the game.

PHONE: 713.387.9273

WEBSITE: ToniHarrisTaylor.com

EMAIL: Toni@ToniHarrisTaylor.com

I dedicate this chapter to my mother, Joyce Jenkins, the first Drastic Stepper I've ever known.

Today I'm in the hot seat. I'm being interviewed by my friend and my publisher, Mr. Marvin D. Cloud, who is publishing this book, Viral Networking for Drastic Results. Thank you, Marvin, for putting me in the hot seat and taking the lead.

Thank you for the opportunity to talk to you and to get inside your brain so that we can share some of this wealth of knowledge that you have about networking with the readers. Toni, who are you, and what do you do?

I am the CEO, Founder and head coach for Drastic Results Marketing and Sales Coaching. Drastic Results helps service-based entrepreneurs that sell their expertise to get known, get connected, and get paid. My uniqueness is I am the Coach that Connects™. In 2019, that became true because I purchased a Network in Action franchise where I bring business owners together to build relationships so that they can help each other grow. Drastic Results and Network in Action was a match made in heaven. At my last conference, I did a talk about accessorizing your dress. I was speaking about adding those business models that would accessorize your main theme. But then I got to thinking about my coaching and Network in Action, and it's like a skirt and blouse or a pair of pants and a shirt. That's how well they go together. It has changed, not just my life, but with the entire Drastic Results and Network in Action Global Partner's family.

I've watched you for the last 10 years that we've known each other. How did the idea come about for your business?

I was a financial advisor from 2000 to 2012. When my husband Robert, passed away, I wanted to do my own thing. The financial services industry was very good to me. It's where drastic was born because suffice it to say I had to be drastic to be successful in that business. I fell out of love with the business because of the compliance restrictions, and I knew I had a bigger passion for helping small business owners to grow. But I didn't know how I would accomplish it. I never talk about it, but I got my degree in entrepreneurship. Getting that degree struck up my passion for entrepreneurs. I left the financial services business and started contracting with Constant Contact. I loved marketing and email marketing. The one thing I discovered was that entrepreneurs love what they do. They just don't want to market it or sell it. Once I realized there was a pain point with entrepreneurs, I developed a niche, a target, and that's how I really got started. In 2016, I was a top five sales reps in the world for Constant Contact. Constant Contact got bought out by a big company that pulled the rug out from under us and drastically decreased the compensation plan. It devastated me. It took me 3 years until NIA came into my life to get my legs back under me. That was a painful time in my business.

But you didn't quit.

I did not quit. I thought about it. I interviewed for jobs, but I did not quit. It was painful. That was probably one of the cloudiest times in my career, in my business, because I just didn't know which way to go.

You started over, but what made you start networking?

My networking started when I was in financial services. They promoted me to management and part of my job was to recruit new financial advisors. I needed to network to find prospects. I started networking, because everybody says, "You have to network." I started showing up at events, passing out a bunch of business cards, and nothing would happen. I was frustrated because I combed my hair, I put on my face, I was nice, and nobody would follow up with me. So, I hired a coach in 2005. I remember it was $6,000 for an eight-week course. Did you hear me? $6,000 for an eight-week course in 2005, and she promised to teach me how to network. I was desperate. I went into my 401k and withdrew the money. I invested in myself.

I tell you that was the best investment I've ever made in my business. She taught me what I needed to know about how to network. But why did I start networking? Because I didn't want to knock on doors or do cold calls. I'm a Jehovah's Witness and I don't want to knock on doors for my business. I don't have a big budget for advertising. The only thing I knew to do was to network. That's how it got started.

There's a lot of emotions when it comes to networking and you know, either you love it, or you hate it. Where do you fall?

You know where I fall. I love networking, but it wasn't always that way. There was a time I dreaded it because I would say I'm going to these events and I'm meeting people, but nothing's happening. I had to learn to love it when I learned to do it right.

Well, let me ask you this. Since in the last couple of years we've had the pandemic and other things ... how do you feel about virtual networking?

I love virtual networking. In fact, my NIA business has expanded to bring on seven leaders and by the end of 2023, I will have 20 leaders running virtual groups. Why do I love virtual networking? I love virtual networking because it expands my borders to nowhere. I had a call earlier this week with someone in Israel. The problem is most people don't know how to do it, so they still feel like it's a waste of time. They go and click on Zoom; they see a bunch of squares, and then what? What I teach is, the then what. What do you do after you get there? I love virtual networking. I'll give a couple of tips on making it better. You must be there. So, show up. Show up means turning the camera on. I am dressed from the waist up. I got lashes on. My makeup is on. I put my hair on. I put my earrings on because I want to look good. First impressions still matter. I go to so many events and people still don't turn their cameras on. That doesn't make any sense. Turn the camera on!

What is it about being an entrepreneur that drives you? You said there were a couple of times you thought about going to get a job.

Let me be clear. In 2019, when NIA came into my life, I had interviewed for two jobs, and I was a shoo-in for both of them. I started looking for a job, not because I wasn't making money. I was looking for a retirement strategy, but inside I didn't want a job.

Why do I stay an entrepreneur today? Because I know that if I can touch, move, and inspire one entrepreneur to be drastic, to learn how to build relationships to feed their family, that can go on for generations. I not only teach the fundamentals of networking and the fundamentals of marketing, but I also teach people to get out of their comfort zone. I give them courage and the wings to get out of their comfort zone. When their children are playing small, guess what they're going to say? My coach Toni said you've got to be drastic because they have developed that mindset for themselves. That's why I stay an entrepreneur. You can't be drastic in corporate because then you're showboating and brown-nosing. You're showing out and they don't appreciate it. So, you can't be drastic in corporate … you've got to play by their rules. So, why I stay an entrepreneur … why I work so hard is because I know I'm leaving a legacy of drastic steppers.

Has there ever been a time that you didn't feel like it, but you showed up and pushed ahead, anyway?

I'm going to let you in on a secret. Everybody sees me as super confident, and I look the part because I work at looking the part and I'm not saying that in a bragging way. It's that I make the effort, so I know I look the part. But there are many times I'm uncomfortable in a new room. I'm going to tell you another secret. I hate to admit it, but I'm going to tell it to the world right now. If I'm not on stage and I'm just an attendee and I'm not playing a role in leadership, I am uncomfortable. I must push myself to stay in the room. I must practice what I teach my clients. I'll show up and then I get super uncomfortable and I'm ready to leave. I know people wouldn't believe that about me, but that's why I must have a role. When I go to conventions and conferences, they are overwhelming for me. I know if it feels that way to me; it feels that way to someone who doesn't know how to make connections. But because I want to be an example for my clients, I push through. The drastic step is for me to stick and stay and push through.

What are some challenges you face in networking?

The one I just shared with you, my own uncomfortable place, and then also making the time. I have to be very intentional. If I see an event, I must book it and schedule it on the spot. Otherwise, it'll get crowded out by other things. The other thing I do is I join groups because I know if I'm in invested in a group, then I'm going to show up. The challenge is finding the time. Then again, when I don't know anyone, I'm uncomfortable too. I know it's hard to believe.

Have you had a big win through networking?

All my wins are through networking. That's the truth. People ask me all the time; how did you find out? Or how do you know? The answer is always networking. The biggest win I've had through networking is meeting my husband. He was a referral. Everything I teach led me to get a referral to Gary. Networking changes lives. It not only changes your business, but it changes lives. You meet friends. When you're in corporate, your coworkers are your friends and create community.

Entrepreneurship can be lonely because there are no coworkers. Your networks become what your coworkers used to be. That's why Network in Action is so great because my members have become family. Even those that have come and gone are still family. I have two ex-members; one is getting married this year and the other one is a bridesmaid. They met at Network in Action. One has children, the other one doesn't. So, she sits in when the mom can't. You can't pay for that. Networking changes the game.

I guess networking really works.

It really works when you work it, and that's the key.

I see you all over. I think social media is a part of networking. Has it helped you? Has it benefited you to be on it? Tell me about social networking.

Social media is everything. So, here's the deal. Social media is an extension of networking, meeting someone in person or virtually. I'm the queen of one-to-ones. When you go to a networking event, you must schedule one-to-ones. Social media keeps you connected after the one-to-ones.

When people meet with you one-to-one, if they're not ready to buy from you today; social media really keeps that relationship and that connection.

Social media has been a big help?

Let me tell the story of how I met Gary. As I mentioned, I'm one of Jehovah's Witnesses. Most people don't know that about us, but we have parties. There was a time, right after my coma, when they invited me to a party. I wasn't really feeling like going out, but my mother wanted to go, and it was a good time for me to get my energy up and go out, so I showed up. When I showed up, there was a young man there from a congregation that I was a part of, but I didn't expect to see him, so I go over and say hello to a group of young men holding up the wall. One of them, Johnny, struck up a conversation, and he said to me, "I'm looking for a wife." Whom do you know? He didn't know he was talking to the networking queen. I said, my daughter and her friends are in your age group. Why don't I schedule a game night? He agreed. I asked, "Are you on Facebook?" He said, "Yes." I said, "Great, let's get connected." We connected that night on Facebook. He gave me his information, and I set up a game night three weeks later and he came. Now, I'm going to pause right here and say three marriages came out of that one game night! (So, I know something about making connections!) As it turns out, he wasn't interested in anybody at the game night party. We took that opportunity to do our one-to-one. We talked about relationships. I asked him, what are you looking for? As a widow at that time, he asked me, what are you looking for? Are you open to being married again? He said, "If I meet someone, I'm going to let you know." It turns out that he met a young lady that night at that same party. Later that year, I saw engagement pictures posted on Facebook. He got engaged. When they posted the pictures on social media, it turns out that Gary knows Johnny's fiancé. Gary called her family and said, everybody's finding somebody but GT. The fiancé turns to Johnny and says, "Whom do you know?" Because we had stayed connected on Facebook, he told her, "I think I might know somebody." He sent me a text by Messenger and asked, "Are you interested in meeting somebody?" I said, "Yes" and the rest, as they say, is history.

Let me recap. I showed up when I didn't feel like it. I met somebody and connected with him on social media, had a one-to-one, and was trying to give to him before he could give to me. He was looking for somebody; I organized a game night. I was attempting to give it to him first. Then, because we stayed connected on social media, he remembered me and gave me a referral to Gary. That's networking in a nutshell.

What mistakes do you see most entrepreneurs make when they go to a networking event?

Trying to sell, not trying to establish a relationship, being aggressive, and being all about themselves. The other mistake is leaving with a pocket or purse full of business cards that they aren't going to follow up with and the other people aren't going to follow up either. My tip is to get people on your calendar on the spot. Stop trying to follow up with people after the fact, because what happens is even when you attempt to follow up on your call, your email, you get no response. It makes you wonder why the heck they come to an event if they don't want to connect? Get them on the calendar on the spot. I'm intentional and drastic to leave every event with three to five appointments. Stop leaving events with business cards that nobody's going to do anything with.

That's that's your number one tip?

That's my number one tip.

Exactly what does it mean to show up? I mean, do you mean just come into the room?

Well, that's the start. My saying is show up, be up, follow up to blow up. What it means to show up is to get there. Put your energy on and stand out as different. Don't blend in with the crowd. What makes you different? Really try to help somebody before you get help. Ask people, what are you doing? What are you working on? How can I help you? That's what it means to show up.

Then you said to follow up. What is your best follow-up tip?

Don't follow up. Get them on your calendar. My second best follow-up tip is after the one-to-one is completed, to connect with them on social media. Be intentional in your social media. Put them on your email list. Have a drip campaign so they can keep seeing your name in their inbox. Yes, inboxes are overrun. Mine is more than overrun, but I see every email that comes in because I must accept it or reject it. It just reminds me that the person is there. Having systems for follow-up is very important.

I know you are not just a national personality; you are an international personality. How has networking helped you to go viral?

I looked up the definition of viral. It says you are viral when people are talking about you when you're not in the room. Many people think going viral is millions of views or millions of likes. It's not that. Going viral is when someone else is talking about you because of your reputation because you've served them in some way. Networking has certainly helped me to build relationships and get clients that will say my name when I'm not around.

Do you have a favorite networking quote or quote about networking?

Yes, my own quote, "Show up, be up, follow up, to blow up!" That's my favorite. My second favorite is Zig Ziglar's quote. "You can have everything you want if you help enough people get what they want." Since NIA came into my life, I've seen that exponentially in my business. I make introductions every single day. In fact, when I'm not making introductions, I feel like something is wrong. Let me find somebody I can introduce. This last year, 2021, financially was unbelievable. It's because I believe Network in Action has given me the platform to do exactly what Zig Ziglar said, help as many people as I can get what they want.

Do you have any final thoughts you can offer to entrepreneurs who are hesitant to network?

My best advice is to get a coach and here's why. Coaches give you courage. If you're left to your own devices, you will talk yourself out of every opportunity. But when you are investing in a coach and that coach is pushing you in a direction, you're going to go in that direction or waste your money. My best advice is to invest in a coach who can push you in the right direction.

I know you are a phenomenal coach. I know many of your clients. You've helped me tremendously through the years that I've known you. But one thing that I never really focused on until the event that you had last November, and that was that you have a coach, and you have coaches. To me, just the fact that the coach has a coach is mind-boggling. What you're saying is that everybody needs a coach.

Everybody needs a coach. Here's the deal, Marvin. We're like that horse with the blinders, and when we are in our business, we can only see as far as we can see. The coach can see what's going on around you and give you guidance so that your blinders don't get in the way. The best of the best athletes have coaches. Serena has a coach. Tiger has a coach. All winners have a coach. I remember the year LeBron won the championship in Cleveland. They went a few weeks without a coach, and they were going crazy trying to figure out who was going to coach them. They know how to dribble and shoot the ball. They wanted one because a coach can see what you can't and every time you're going to your next level, whatever it is, they can't do it on your own. You cannot. It is important that all entrepreneurs get a good coach. Now, there are many people calling themselves coaches out there that aren't good. They take people's money. Find the coach that has a great reputation and does the work.

GLENN WALKER: FINANCIAL SERVICES PROFESSIONAL

GLENN WALKER is married to his college sweetheart and a father of three. His passion for financial planning stems from losing his dad two days after graduating high school. He saw his mother struggle financially putting the pieces back together and knew he needed to do something to help families like his own. Glenn has over a decade in Financial Services experience and has completed his formal education from Sam Houston State University where he received his bachelor's in business and Finance. Later Glenn continued his education at Rice University where he successfully completed the course work of CERTIFIED FINANCIAL PLANNER™.

PHONE: 832.286.6576

WEBSITE: FinancialGuide.com
EMAIL: GlennWalker@FinancialGuide.com

I dedicate this to my wife and kids. Also those who aspire to become Entrepreneurs. Great people do not become great on their own, neither do they keep their greatness to themselves.

I am super excited to introduce to you and present to others, Mr. Glenn Walker. I appreciate you taking advantage of being a part of the book project, and we are going to talk about your networking. Also, we are going to talk about how networking for you is going viral. First, who are you and what do you do?

I am Glenn Walker, I just turned 31 years of age. I am married to my college Sweetheart going on 6 years and we have 3 perfect kids together Lily, Glenn IV, and Chloe. I am also the proud owner of Greater Wealth Financial Solutions. I am a student of the business my expertise is in Financial Planning. Toni, I have been in the industry over 10 years now and I see myself doing this another 30, 40 years, so I am just getting started. Eventually I will need an exit strategy, but for now I am just enjoying the process. So, as a student of the business I really love what I do and am enthusiastic about helping people and about making a financial change in my client's futures.

You are specifically about helping young families because you have a young family. Tell us a little bit about your family and why family is your passion.

Family is everything to me. I grew up in a strong two parent household. 2010 was a rough year for me but it was also a defining year. That is the year I graduated high school, which also was the same year that my grandfather and father were both diagnosed with cancer. At this point my mom and dad both quit their jobs to deal with this illness that overwhelmed my family. Needless to say, all of their benefits stayed with the company. Then on June 8th two days after I graduated high school my dad passed away. When he passed, my dad had no personal life insurance policy, to help pay off the house we currently lived in or support my sister and I to go to college, or even help cover funeral costs. So, my family suffered twice the loss of my father and the loss of the security that my parent's income provided. Losing my father was devastating and then feeling the financial pressures of the world I felt vulnerable.

A few years later my mom did a short sale on the home we grow up in. At the point I jumped into finance to learn how about money works. At this point I found a mission that I believed in, that is to help my clients to become debt free, properly protected, and financially independent.

The reason I help young families is because when we graduate college most students have a ton of student loan debt. Then we go into more debt purchasing a new car or we buy our first house. Sometimes that is even before we get married. One spouse has student loans marries another spouse who has student loans on top of getting a mortgage. There are so many decisions that are bombarding us all at one time. There is an overwhelming number of financial situations that is on the minds of graduates. Young adults just starting their careers are not properly educated on how to manage a sudden increase in financial pay overnight, all or some of them do not have the proper guidance helping them, like a money expert.

I see this all the time young people make financial mistakes that sets their success back for years, what sets young people back financially in addition to wasting money is wasting time. One of the worse things that young family can do is get into consumer debt. Debt limits the person as far as what they can do with their families on vacations, also what they can do in their future when it comes to certain jobs. It impacts so much, Toni. It really does.

This will air and be published much later, but I am just excited for your family. I remember when you came to me, you had just quit the job to become an entrepreneur. So how did becoming an entrepreneur come about?

Honestly, it came about when I was in high school. I did not know business I wanted to start. I invited some friends over to brainstorm what business venture we can start that did not go far at the time but looking at them now they both work for themselves. Becoming an entrepreneur for me was a calling. Back in high school I did not even know what an entrepreneur was or what they did. I just remember telling my neighbors, I am going to be an entrepreneur, I will have my own business that was well over 12 years ago. Even while I was in high school and middle school, I would go around cutting my neighbors yards and trimming their bushes, I would also clear out old garden beds and eventually started working with my cousin who was an entrepreneur to help clear construction sites.

I always had an entrepreneurial work ethic and mindset and even while working on past jobs, I always would think about what can I do for myself? Because what I desired was freedom. I like the freedom that I have right now, just being able to be at home with my wife and my kids and not have to ask anybody or say, "Hey, can I take time off for vacation," but truly having freedom. Because I have a vision for my life and that is to be able to travel, that is to be able to spend quality time with my family, because life is so short.

There is nothing wrong with a job. We need to be careful we do not get caught up into the rat race and live from paycheck to paycheck. I feel like that for me at least, I am not speaking for anybody else. It takes discipline to work for yourself and run your own schedule, if we do not have the discipline to do it ourselves a job would be more than happy to provide us that structure. When I was working at the bank, I would look out the window and watch cars pass by and ask, "Where are they going? I want to go." I did not want to go to the same building every day. Entrepreneurship is exciting and it takes a lot of mental toughness, but I wanted the freedom, it is not about the money, but it's about the freedom but freedom is not free.

You start your business. What made you say, I have to start networking?

Because I believe in the ideology to be great, I must be around other great people. People that are great do not become great on their own, neither do they keep their greatness to themselves. That is the saying I told myself years ago. I knew that for me to do something big, that I had to have a team, I had to be around people, because that is what it is all about. Business is not about an actual building or being in an office space, but it is about building people, building quality relationships with people. Once you start building relationships with people, that is when you start building a business. Because right now, because of the networking, my business has been primarily referrals and this is only in the first year. Most businesses do not become referral based within the first year. It takes a couple years for business owners to get their name out there, to start building credibility with people. But, within the first year, a lot of my business has been from referrals, which has been a result from networking!

When it comes to networking, there are so many emotions. People either love it or they hate it. So where do you fall on the networking scale?

It depends on what day it is. Truly I am naturally an introvert if I am being honest. So, when I go to a networking event, I must mentally prepare myself to be around a social environment because after leaving a social environment, I am mentally drained about being around so many people. I had learned to monitor myself when I go to networking events. When I go to a networking event, I have to say, "Okay, what is my goal?" I do not go to a networking event without having the goal first. How many people am I going to talk to? How many meetings am I going to set? Because if I go there trying to talk to the whole room, I will not be successful. To be successful in networking I must be intentional and limit myself from burn out. I must monitor myself like a parking meter, I must measure my success and social energy.

Since the pandemic, and you and I met during the pandemic, virtual networking has become more popular. So, what tips can you share to maximize virtual networking?

My tips to maximize virtual networking is to make sure you have your virtual business tools set up and ready to go. What I mean by that is when you are on zoom make sure you have a good webcam. Purchase a quality webcam that should be a given. Secondly, have your copy and paste for all your contact information, like your phone number, email address, website, so that way it is already there to share with others in the group. Learn how to stand out and be authentic and not robotic people want to connect with a real person when they network virtually. You must be ready for the opportunity. Have your social media set up, like your Facebook, LinkedIn, another popular site to use is Linktree (Linktr.ee). So, people can follow you and find you. Virtual networking is a little bit easier if you are prepared, you only must set it up one time and then make changes as you go. Once you set up your website, social media the only thing you must do is copy and paste and you're good to go.

You have talked about the freedom, flexibility of being an entrepreneur. But Glenn, I know because you and I office in the same space and you have sat on my couch more than once. I know this journey for the first year has not been easy. What has kept you in the game? What has kept you from going to get a job?

Toni, that is a good question. What has kept me from getting a job? I was recently confiding in my wife about how many difficulties and challenges I have faced, she mentioned to me that she noticed a difference in me when I work from the office versus working from home. When I have a difficult season, I have the privilege of taking to mentors like yourself and Roy who also have faced many challenges. It is also good to know that I am not alone and that we are all facing mountains that we are trying to climb.

Next, it is the vision that I have, the vision that I have for my kids, the vision that I have for my life and that vision is to have freedom. It is all about the freedom and I must be very clear about what freedom looks like, for example the vacations I want to experience the exact car I want to drive. I must have an unclouded vision because on the hard days when I want to throw in the towel, which are many days! I must remind myself why I am enduring this pain. To be a successful business owner, you must have grit because there will be many times you question why you are doing this in the first place. Toni, it is finally about faith. It is about knowing that things are going to work out. There is an analogy I love to use. I call it the ram in the bush. Because the closer you get to your goals, the closer you get to your vision, God will start to provide what you need at that time. A lot of times the reason people may not become entrepreneurs is because they cannot see the whole path. They say to themselves, "okay, I'm here and I want to be there," but then they do not see the little streets that it takes to get to their destination. You must take the leap; you must take the first step-in order for everything to fall into place. Entrepreneurship is a faith walk, it has tested me, and it will continue to do so until that is part of the adventure. Faith at the end of each day is all I have to hold onto when my family and friends cannot fix it my problems, I trust that He will never leave me or forsake me. Being an entrepreneur has been the biggest faith journey that I have ever been on so far in my life. So, it is about keeping the faith, staying faithful to your vision, and never giving up.

Tell me about a time that you did not want to show up, you pushed ahead, and you are glad you did.

There was a networking event hosted by my church, I did not want to show up because there was just so much going on at that time. I was dealing with family, work and kids not getting enough sleep because of a newborn. I was overwhelmed with all the responsibilities that I had going on at one time. I still chose to get up and show up. I created a networking goal for myself to limit my energy so I could meet quality people and make strong connections. When I showed up despite my challenges it opens the door for new opportunities to come from it. As a result, for me showing up to an event that I did not want to go to, I meet one of my best clients who has since then referred me to other quality individuals which helped expand my network. My advice, to myself would be I always need to show up the most when I do not feel like it. You must show up the most when you do not feel like it, because that is when you know the breakthrough is right there. There is a book titled, *Three Feet From Gold*. Right when you want to give up, you are right there before the breakthrough you have been waiting on, you must keep going and showing up.

Business is all about compounding. It just compounds on each other. That one person may turn into another person that may turn into another person. What we do in our business compounds on itself, the efforts that we put in. Relationships we build have the potential to compound. Compound interest, I love compound interest Albert Einstein, calls, it "the eighth wonder of the world he who understands it earns it, he who doesn't pays it." Toni, I am telling you, that compound interest is what makes people rich, and it is also what keeps people poor. It is compound interest. It either works for you or it works against you. Especially in relationships, it can work wonders for you in business.

Even though we are figuring out networking. We all have challenges when it comes to networking. What is one of your challenges you have with networking?

Getting in my own head and in my own way. The head trash that I had to overcome about wanting people to like me. As humans we criticize ourselves, worry and over think too much. As an entrepreneur myself, I am in the people business my number one job is to make other people feel comfortable around me. One of the hardest lessons that I had to learn, Toni, is that not everybody is going to like you. Growing up I always imaged that everyone liked me. But one of my mentors told me this and it was the hardest truth that I ever heard, is that "Not everybody is going to like you." Even still to this today, it is hard for me to accept that. I had a reminder of this lesson recently someone came into my office and said, "People are going to look for reasons not to like you." Personally, we cannot control who likes us or not. The most important lesson is to make sure we like the person that we are and are becoming. In business, there is a quote going viral on the internet right now that says, "Sometimes it's easier for a client to become a friend than a friend to become a client." When you go into business for yourself, you will truly start to see who is there for you and who just has the lip service. It is a tough pill to swallow sometimes. But it is what it is. This can be related back into business too. You must sometimes kick people to the side and leave them where they are. Not everybody is going to be a friend and not everybody is going to be a client and we got to be okay with that. Sometimes when you try to make the wrong person a client, they become more trouble than what it is worth. It is better to leave that person alone versus wasting effort and energy to earn their business. I learned it is better to have a smaller client in which we share a great relationship with over a horrible client that I will get paid a lot more money on, but I don't have that relationship with them. I would rather have in the long-term good relationships over major profits with bad relationships. No client is worth sacrificing my peace of mind or self-worth.

Tell me about a time that networking made a significant difference in your business.

Networking is more than just what I can get out of it but also what my network can get from it. Toni you taught me the importance of networking is for my network. I may show up to a networking event and meet someone not for me but that can help benefit someone else that I know. I never know who I will meet that can help change the lives of someone else that I already know.

When you network with other people it opens your mind it allows you to meet with people who otherwise you might have never got to meet and experience diverse cultures and see different ways of thinking. I cannot speak on that enough; networking gives us a different paradigm shift. Our world is so divided and for us to start healing we need to learn how to network and connect with other groups of people. You then start to see business and life from other people's eyes and point of view. You start to see how everything works together and we are not as different as the world would like us to believe.

We see the bigger picture how showing up and networking impacts your business because it impacts your mind. To be a millionaire, you must first become a millionaire in your mind. It is easy to give someone a million dollars I have seen plenty of people squander substantial amounts of money in under a year, if you do not know how money works or accustomed to saving money, how can you do better if you are not taught or exposed? Being around the right people and being in the right environment, which is how networking makes a huge difference in our business, networking helps elevate your mindset and knowledge when you meet the right people. Lastly, you then start to believe by being around people who are successful business owners it makes being in business for yourself obtainable. It gives you a belief that if they can do it so can I, when you network with someone who is successful, they can transfer their knowledge to a beginner.

Social media is a form of networking. How has social media helped you to grow your business?

I am incredibly surprised how many people have reached out to me on social media wanting to do business. Social media is a passive way for our friends and family to stay connected with us. When they see that you have been in business for years then you become the expert in their network. They will begin to reach out and ask question, even some will turn into clients. Social media gives business owners leverage to gain influence over prospects.

Social media is like the new drug. It is addicting. Social media has the power to cause real world change, it has been proven to help unite the world! Social media needs to be used responsibly as business owners. Because you can use social media as 24-hour free advertising. If you have an event coming up, you can post it on social media. If you have a success story, you post it on social media and it is not bragging, but it is about promoting. People are accustomed to being sold every seven seconds. We are always being sold something whether we realize it or not. So social media can be a platform to help us to be able to market our products and services to others. We may not get everybody, but at least people know who we are and what we do, and that is the biggest key. Awareness, making people aware of what you do and who you are.

VALERIA VICK: CONTENT COPYWRITER

VALERIA VICK, owner of Val Vick Content & Copywriting believes content marketing done well guarantees more sales. She is a content marketing strategist and copywriter for entrepreneurs and small businesses. She offers both done-for-you services and coaching for DIY (do-it-yourself) clients.

She creates content that blends elements of brand voice, storytelling, customer experience, and search engine optimization (SEO) to help businesses be visible, recognized, and trusted.

PHONE: 281-757-3057

WEBSITE: ValVickCopywriting.com

EMAIL: Val@ValeriaVick.com

Every choice is guided by faith and family.
Thanks to God and the village assigned to me. #Grateful

Today's guest is one of my favorite clients. I know you're all thinking, *Toni says that about all her clients.* **But Val is really one of my favorite clients. She shows up everywhere, regardless of what's going on in her life. Even in the middle of her storms, she is always there. Because of that, her business has reaped the benefits. So, I'm going to introduce you to Mrs. Val Vick of Val Vick Content & Copywriting. Welcome Val. Tell us in your own words, who you are and what you do.**

My name is Valeria Collier-Vick, but most people shorten it to Val Vick. I magnify the differences of business owners so they can stand out from their competitors. I do that by using marketing content and copy in their digital and print deliverables, such as their website, newsletter, or email campaigns. We help them stand out.

I love that, and I love how you said magnify so they can attract their ideal clients. The written word is part of showing up and Val is amazing. Actually, she is my copywriter and helps me with my newsletters and my website content as well. Thank you, Val. So, Val, you've been through lots of transitions. In fact, Val and I met networking, I want to say in 2008 or 2009. She was in my very first book in 2012. She's been through several iterations of her entrepreneurship journey. Tell us your story and how you landed here as a copywriter.

I'm a licensed professional engineer, a certified project manager, and I've worked in corporate America. I started working in corporate America back in the late seventies. I worked for Exxon after college graduation, and later, I worked for an engineering consulting firm. But I left the consulting firm when our daughter turned 13 years old. We agreed that for her teen years, I would be a stay-at-home mom. So, I became a "soccer mom" and an entrepreneur. I got a real estate license. I started a travel business and several other businesses. I was that serial entrepreneur. But I realized very quickly that leaving corporate America to start your own thing is a whole different ball game. Nobody knows you. You're invisible. I learned networking is critical to becoming visible. That was the first step toward visibility. That's where I met you, on that first journey. I ended up focusing on the travel business. I did real estate because my mom owns commercial property, and so I kept my license. But the travel business was the one I loved. In fact, I worked with your daughter when she started a travel business. I kept growing my travel business from 2008 through 2019. Then the pandemic happened and all travel stopped. Travel was the one area where everybody felt you couldn't go anywhere. You couldn't do anything. I only get paid when people travel. That meant no income. I had to pivot. I circled back to something that I knew how to do, which was to write sales and marketing materials. That's where copywriting comes in. That is the copywrite with W-R-I-T-E not R-I-G-H-T. Some people say to me, "I have a book. I want to get it copyrighted." I have to explain, "That's not what I do, but let me help you find someone." My writing is all about helping you get your marketing messages out there so you can attract, retain, and convert your ideal customer.

We've learned through our coaching that only 2% to 3% of people are ready to purchase from you the day they meet you. It's probably not even that. It's important … it's imperative … that you stay in front of those people so that when they're ready, you're right there. That's what Val does. She helps you to stay connected to those prospects so that when they're ready, you're still in front of them. So Val, what made you start networking?

First of all, I got an invitation to join someone at a networking event. Let's be honest, even in corporate America, you're networking all of the time, either inside the company or outside. I always had a role in business development in the consulting company I worked for, so I was networking with the corporate name behind me. I would go to conferences, and I would speak at conferences. I was being published and speaking at technical conferences as an engineer. We would have mixers and socials. I was networking for the company. Networking for myself was very different. That, I think, is what I didn't really understand. I knew about the concept, but it was different when it was for me. My first invitation was to a women's networking event. That was my first time going to a networking event representing myself - networking for myself. I could see that it could make a difference, getting to talk to people and letting them know you're here. Nobody knows you exist unless you're out there.

When it comes to networking, there are so many emotions. Some people love it. Some people hate it. I know where you are on the scale now, but where were you when you first started networking? What were your emotions around it?

You say, you know where I am now, but I'm not sure you do. I'm one of those outgoing introverts. I can turn it on, but if you ask me, do you want to go out and network, I'd say no. I'd rather stay home and read my Kindle or watch my Hallmark movies. I really like being by myself. I don't really want to go out there. I understand the importance of networking. When I turn on, I'm one of the best at turning on. So, I can show up and I can be a networker, but I don't really like it. I can't have a successful business without networking. I don't love networking, but I've learned to respect it.

Speak to the introverts then. What do you do to turn yourself on, to make it happen, even when you don't feel like it?

I think it's a mindset. It's truly a mental exercise. I learned how to be outgoing. As an 11-year-old child with acne, being 5'11", wearing a size 11 shoe, with glasses and braces, I wasn't trying to be visible. I was visible because I couldn't help it, but I was very shy and insecure about my physical appearance. So in my teen years, I started coming out a little more. I learned how to be outgoing. I think people who are shy need a reason to shift or change. They can learn how to be outgoing. I got positive reinforcement for being outgoing, so I worked on it. I would tell people who are introverts like me, but they're more on the shy side, you've got to work on your mental issues and recognize there's something that caused you to be fearful and shy. It's really something you can practice. So here's what I'd suggest if you aren't naturally outgoing. I think being outgoing is learned. If you haven't learned how to be outgoing, I think you should go into a networking situation realizing that most people want you to be successful. Most people want to get to know you and most people don't want you to be anybody you're not. So go ahead and go in and be a little shy, a little hesitant, but take that first step and say,

"Hi, I'm Val. What's your name? Then if you can't think of anything else to say, then say, "How can I help you?"

That's it, there you go. You've got to show up regardless. Here's the thing about networking. Everybody's there for the same reason ... to help each other. Some people are there to see what they can get for themselves, but most people have a helping posture. There are a lot of other people like you who are uncomfortable, shy, don't know what they're saying, afraid to make a mistake and they show up anyway. Thank you for those words of wisdom. That was awesome. So virtual networking since the pandemic has become more popular, and I know that you've built your business pretty much since the pandemic strictly on virtual networking. What tips would you give someone on virtual networking?

Similar to in-person networking you show up and that means turning your camera on. I see a lot of people attending a virtual event and leaving their camera off. Their name shows up, but they're not visible. People aren't as receptive or interested in talking to a blank screen with a printed name. That's the first step. Show up and turn your camera on. Then when you're on camera, don't get distracted with other things. Put the phone away, don't let the kids and the dog come in and hang out with you. People think it's cute, but it's only cute for five seconds. Remove distractions and just like with physical in-person networking, be present and really engaged. One of my pet peeves are the people who treat networking like speed dating. They're trying to see how many people they can meet. They rush through it. They're not really listening to you. It's very superficial. They're seeing 'how many cards I can collect'? However, they miss the whole point. Without that engagement, there's no connection. Give people your attention, and really listen and be sincere about it. If you're not going to be sincere, you shouldn't join in.

Your driving force to becoming an entrepreneur was that you wanted to be home for your daughter's most important years, her teenage years, for Shannon. Shout out to Shannon. But now, you could get a job. I mean Harvey does well. He's a geologist, he's good. So what's your key driving force for continuing to be an entrepreneur?

You're right, and I have asked, "why do I still do this at my age?" I could stop ... I'm prepared for retirement ... and I'm waiting for the 65 Medicare Mama thing. But meanwhile, my drive is still our daughter. She's an actor, and if you're not familiar with that business, it's tough. She was one of those kids who wanted to be an entertainer since she was two years old. I'm not kidding, it was really early. But we asked her to please wait and not ask us to do the childhood actor journey. Even in her teen years, we told her, if you wait and go to college, we'll help you. We support her. She works with me, so she has flexibility in her schedule for her auditions. I'm doing this because of my love for my daughter.

I love that, and you guys now are a great team in your business while she's living her dream. So thank you for continuing to be an entrepreneur and having a big why.

So now, tell me about a time you didn't want to show up, you pushed through, and you're glad you did.

I have a recent example of that. Sometimes we'll assume the group that we're going to meet with may not be a good match because it's not obvious that the connections are going to be the right ones. We assume a lot. We think we know who's right and who's not. We don't. If you think about it, it's not about that person, sometimes it's about who that person knows. Any maybe not who they know, but who they know that knows others; that six degrees of separation concept. I recently went to an event you invited me to. It was a luncheon. In my mind, luncheons aren't necessarily good networking places. You're sitting there at a table eating. How do you make connections at an event like that? That was my mindset going into the lunch. Well, I went to that luncheon. I sat next to a lady. We talked, exchanged information and then later I met another lady that I connected with - both of those people became clients. The other reason I didn't want to go was because I didn't want to put on clothes and shoes.

That stops people from showing up. Especially women. They don't want to put themselves together. But look at you; you showed up, you got two clients, those clients will give you referrals. Networking is the one marketing prospecting strategy that snowballs when you know what to do. Now we all have challenges with networking. Tell me what your main challenge is.

For me, it's the commitment to show up and be up because I'm an introvert. It's tough. Sometimes I have to come home and decompress. I don't want to talk to anybody for about a day. It really is draining for me. Sometimes, I think one of the challenges with me is the follow up when I've met so many people, making sure I not only make that first try to schedule that first one-to-one follow up, but following up more after that. That's how I think the importance of the drip campaigns that we're talking about in coaching is important because not everybody will automatically become part of your community, so you've got to keep at it a little bit more. That's one of the things I haven't been as effective with.

You shared a story about how you showed up when you didn't feel like it. But tell me about where networking's made a huge difference in your business.

I think your concept of viral networking is what's made the difference in the business because I've had several situations where the person I met wasn't the person that ended up becoming an integral part of my community or becoming a client. Again, the person I met knew somebody who knew somebody. That's been the key networking benefit for my business growth.

So social media is a form of networking. In fact, social media got us back here. Tell me how social media has helped you to grow your business.

You got on the live and you said something, and I commented, and you said let's catch up. That was huge. I model what you do as much as possible, so I started doing that. I say, "Let's catch up," when somebody comments now. I get the most reactions on my posting when I'm talking about my travels, because people know me as the travel person, and they're like, "I want to be like you when I grow up," or they'll reach out to me. I have had several people say, "Hey, I see you doing something else also."

So what mistakes have you seen entrepreneurs make when it comes to networking? Then what tip would you give?

I think the mistake some make is they treat it like a way to get sales. Networking is not about sales. It's about the connections. Don't go in with the expectation that you're going to make a sale or find somebody who's ready to buy from you, because that's not what it's for. It's for meeting new people to make new connections and create and develop new relationships because business will come from a string of relationships. That would be the mistake. The tip from that is to go in knowing that your only reason to network is to meet people and sincerely engage. Find out what they need and how you can help. Often you figure out how you can help each other. I believe that the sales conversation is going to show up with the right person at the right time. Part of your opportunity is not being afraid to have that conversation. The real opportunity is recognizing that this is the right time with this person, because you cannot sell to me if I don't know, like, or trust you. There's too many of you that do the same thing. If you were the only one who had this piece of bread, maybe you could sell it to me. But let's be honest, I know there are a billion people who have the same piece of bread, and I don't have to buy it from you.

What does it mean to show up?

Show up by putting on some clothes, even if you're on zoom, and just get there so you can show up. There's plenty of reasons you could say I can't do it. The "be up" is important because there are things always going on in our lives and you might be in your feelings. But for the most part, if you're going to show up, you need to "be up" and and turn it on. I'm not saying be fake. You need to be authentic. But even if you're reserved, you need to be engaged. That's what I think being up means.

What's your best strategy for follow up?

I tell people, even if it's only for 15 minutes, we can do an initial touch base. But typically the 30 minute follow up conversation is really a good first step. You figure out then if there's somebody you know, we can introduce each other to, or we at least understand how to listen for a match. That's the question I ask, "How would I recognize somebody who would be a good introduction for you?" I get them to describe that person and situation. The next step, you invite them to join your community some kind of way with a free gift or your drip campaign, your newsletter. I also offer if you need my help, I'd love to help you.

It's going to be a whole year of connections that have gone viral, but it's nice to have that visual. Networking

keeps giving. What's your favorite quote around networking or connecting?

Networking works when you work it.

What are the final thoughts you would offer to someone who is hesitant to network?

My final thoughts and suggestion would be even if you're afraid or uncomfortable, still do it. Like anything else, until you practice doing it, it won't become second nature or comfortable. Networking is learned. Nobody's born knowing how to do it well. Learn and practice, it's going to happen. It's going to make a difference. It's going to change your life.

MARIETTA WILLIS: CEO & BUSINESS CREDIT SPECIALIST

MARIETTA WILLIS, the founder of several area businesses including Strategic Growth Alliance 366 LLC offering physical/virtual office space, access to advanced-technology conference rooms, fitness center, etc. Together with Richmond Capital, she provides services in business coaching, capital, credit, digital marketing, national and international television advertisement streams for emerging businesses.

PHONE: 346.229.5815

WEBSITE: SGA366.com

EMAIL: info@SGA366.com

This section is dedicated "In Loving Memory" to my Mom, "Rushie Thomas-Floyd," my biggest champion to push me to be the best of who I am. I also thank my children, and my brothers and sisters, who are always supportive in everything I do. I love you all, dearly.

We have another fabulous author of the *Viral Networking for Drastic Results* book, Miss Marietta Willis. Welcome, Marietta. When you look up the definition of serial entrepreneur, her picture is there. So she has a lot of stuff going on. In your own words, who are you and what do you do?

Well, Toni, my name is Marietta Willis. I am a serial entrepreneur. I've been an entrepreneur for over 20 years. I am currently the CEO and owner of Encore Consulting and IT, Richmond Capital Solutions, the CEO of Strategic Growth Alliance 366 and 366 SkyLounge and Event Center.

She's my landlord too. There you go. She's got a lot of things going on, but I will tell you the foundation of everything Mari has going on is what? Networking. How did your businesses come about?

Well, to kind of give a ballpark overview. It started years ago for my kids. I was a single parent and I wanted to make sure that I had additional income that would allow me to take care of my kids with the comfort I wanted. I looked into a few options to make extra money and started my business doing taxes. Although I started out with a tax business, I have owned several other successful businesses over the years. I have always had something on the side of my full-time job.

I know because we are right here together that you took the drastic step and left a corporate job recently. How does that feel?

That feels great, because I wake up to my own tune. I'm not worried about what time I'm getting up and running out the door. Although I still am on a schedule for myself, it is my schedule. The long hours I work is to build my own legacy not someone else's. That's what makes the big difference.

I've talked to a lot of people in this book, but you are the one that is the true introvert. You're the one person that is like that quiet, very reserved and introverted. In this conversation, I want you to really tailor to the introverts in the room. Why did you start networking?

I started networking because as an introvert, I didn't really know a whole lot of people first of all. I knew what it is I wanted to do. I knew that I could help people with what I do. So I knew networking was the next step. So I joined a chamber of commerce and that's kind of where I got started with networking. It was hard, but I did it.

Not only is she an introvert, she's also very analytical. She's not the most, and I'm not saying this in a negative way, so you all don't hear it that way, but she's just not a people person and it's OK, that's fine. I will give her my contracts and my numbers any day. I know she's got that, because that is my weakness. For you to decide that networking was the right way to build your business, even though it was so outside your comfort zone, that's very drastic and admirable. So when it comes to networking, there are so many emotions. People love it or they hate it. Where do you fall on the networking meter?

When I started, I hated it. I literally hated it because I had anxieties. I would go to a networking event and I might get to the door and turn around and go home. That's how bad it was for me. It took some time, but I pushed myself and decided, okay, I'm going to go in, I'm going to talk to three people and then I'll leave. That's what I did initially. That's how I kind of pushed myself into it. I went in, talked to three people and I left, but now I can actually go to a networking event and talk to everyone.

To watch her work now is amazing. We will get into this a little bit later, but just watching you evolve even in the last two years since we've been connected has been wonderful. Wow! Virtual networking has become more

popular since the pandemic. What tips would you give an entrepreneur around virtual networking?

It certainly makes things a little easier than running out to the networking event. It cuts down on the time it takes to actually do the networking and because you don't have to run out, you don't have to come back. It's one hour or 30 minutes, whatever you've set aside. It makes it a little bit easier just to have a conversation and you're in a room by yourselves.

Now you talked about your driving force to becoming an entrepreneur. You needed a side hustle to support your family. We've all had those peaks and valleys. What is your driving force now to staying an entrepreneur?

Now it's just what I love to do. I love helping people. I love seeing people win and I love being that person that can help you get there. It's always been something that I love to do. My first networking, like I said, with the chamber of commerce, I met someone there who has helped me along the way too with that. But she had a driving force for helping people as well. So we kind of got to be real good friends for that reason. Helping people is really my driving force.

You do a great job at helping all of us up here at SGA 366. We appreciate you and your leadership. Thank you. Tell me about a time that you didn't want to show up. You pushed ahead and you're glad you did it.

I guess I'll have to go back to that chamber of commerce because that was it. I pushed myself to network and to talk to people, I actually met the person who became a very good friend, but not only became a very good friend, she was my admin. I'd often say that if it weren't for her, I wouldn't get paid because I was that person that liked to help. I might do the job and might forget to send you an invoice, but she helped me keep that on track. So it was very helpful for me to have her as my admin.

Tell me about your challenges with networking, even though you love it now, what are your challenges? We all have them.

The biggest challenge is time. Making the time to do the networking, as you already know. But, of course, it is necessary. So you really do have to find that time because if you stop networking, you stop growing.

There you go. It's a balance, right? It's all about making the time. Right? Now, tell me about a time that networking has made a big difference in your business.

Oh, that's the easy one. Two years ago I was in a networking group where I met my partner, my current partner, Sonja Lowe. Again, being that introvert, we didn't really speak a whole lot, but I did see something in her that drew me to her. I felt like she had something I needed. I took the time to talk with her, speak with her, even have some one on ones with her. I knew that there was something there and as busy as she was, at that time too, she spent time with me. So in the time that we found that networking group was not something that was good for either of us and we broke away from that. We came together after that and literally, almost immediately decided we were going to be working together. For me, this is one of the biggest things because what we're doing now has allowed me to retire from corporate America.

Honestly, you and Sonja need to make a TV show or not a show, but a video, because you guys and your connection

and how it has become evolutionary in your lives and business is like the picture of networking. It's almost like a fairy tale or almost like a love story. It really is.

Yes. I can agree with that. Because it's almost unlikely that the two of us would be together. We are totally different.

Now we live in a different world, so let's be clear. Sonja's married to her king and Marietta is looking for hers. Your story with networking is like a love story. Even though it hasn't been perfect, lots of peaks and valleys, you all are hanging in there and committed to each other and the process. I love your story. We need to do something with that because it really is the picture of what's possible when you show up. Social media is a form of networking. How has social media helped you to grow your business?

For the most part, most of what my marketing is on social media. Just connecting with different people. I find a lot of people are connecting with me even without me even trying, but that has been the biggest piece of marketing for us.

I know the 366 Lounge, right? It gets a lot of publicity through social media, but the other thing is I know social media keeps you connected to so many people. Those people are showing up again in your life. What mistakes do you see entrepreneurs make when it comes to networking and what's your best tip for them?

I guess the biggest mistake I can see is one that I make, not showing up on a consistent basis. I mean, I show up, but sometimes it's not consistent. You do have to be consistent because how else will a person get to know you? Had I not pushed myself to go to the chamber at that time, there are a few people that I know now, including yourself, that

I probably would not have connected with. So definitely being consistent.

The tip is to show up, even when you're an introvert, even when you're in your head about it, when you get to the door and you want to turn around, walk through the door anyway. Very good. So what does it mean though Mari, for you to show up or for an entrepreneur to show up? So I'm here, right? I'm at the event I walk through the door. What else does an entrepreneur need to do in order to show up?

You talk, you communicate. But most importantly, you get that one to one. As you've taught us, you do that right then and there, don't wait till you get home. You do it right then and there, because one of my mistakes is I would wait till I get home. Then maybe, or maybe not, that call might not get made. That one to one didn't happen a lot of times but making that appointment right then and there is probably the most important.

That's a consistent theme throughout this book, because everybody has said "book it on the spot," which is still drastic even though you know it conceptually you understand why it's important. It's still hard to ask for a date on the spot. I'm glad you understand that. My clients, don't leave events without dates, period. It doesn't make sense to show up and then leave with just a business card. Who needs more pieces of paper on their desks? Not one person.

I don't take business cards anymore.

Good for you. In addition to that, do you have any other suggestions for following up?

Follow up the first time is just once, but in order to really get to know a person you want to follow up more than once. At least two or three times just to build a relationship. Not just to talk about business, but to build a relationship. That's important. You may not do anything with that person right now, but you never know what's going to happen down the road.

Because you don't get married on the first date. It's the dates that come after the first date that really solidifies the relationship. So your tip is book more dates, book more engagements, stay connected. Describe how your networking has gone viral.

I guess you can say that a lot of the business that we do now is more of word of mouth, because we haven't actually done a lot of networking, but the word of mouth has been happening. To me, that's viral because that's what you really want in business is to have that word of mouth and the recommendations.

What's your favorite quote around networking or connecting?

Well, Toni, when I was young, my mom used to have speakers in our bedrooms and within those speakers, she had us listening to Zig Ziglar all night long. My quote comes from Zig Ziglar. "You can have everything in life you want, if you will just help enough people get what they want." That has definitely stuck with me along with some of the sounds he made when he was talking. But yes, and that's what we're doing now. That's what our business is all about now, collaboration and helping others. Definitely helping as many as we can and we'll definitely get what you want out of life.

That is my quote. I love that quote, too. It is hanging on my wall. "You can have everything you want in life, if you help enough people get what they want." I want to thank you personally for helping me to get what I want. I am grateful to be a part of your SGA family.

You're welcome.

What final thoughts can you offer an entrepreneur who's hesitant to network?

All I can say is just do it, just be the Nike person, just do it. When you feel like you can't or you don't want to, you really do have to get out of your head, just step inside and see what happens. That's really all you need to do. Just step inside and see what happens. That's how I push myself.

Marketing & Sales Coach | Award Winning Franchisee | International Speaker | Videocast Show Host

"Successful people, take drastic steps to get drastic results, period!"–***Toni Harris Taylor***

I am a marketing and sales coach and a passionate international speaker. I'm known as The Networking Queen and The Coach that Connects™. My company, Drastic Results Marketing and Sales Coaching helps entrepreneurs get known, get connected, and get paid! I teach the how-to of leveraging branding, networking, and speaking to attract clients magnetically to grow to six figures and beyond! I also have a videocast where I interview successful entrepreneurs to touch, move and inspire the audience to stay in the game.

I also own a Network in Action franchise where I help business owners to grow through networking, education, community, and business development. I am a multi-unit, award-winning franchise owner. As a franchisee, they have awarded me the 2019 Rookie of the Year, and 2021 Brand Ambassador awards. Dr. George C. Fraser of the Power Networking Conference awarded me the 2022 Power Networker of the Year Award.

On a personal note, I have overcome many obstacles, including being a two-time widow and coming back from near-death after spending 10 days in a coma. I am married, a mother to two, and a stepmother to three adult children. I am a grandmother to seven (five boys, and two girls). I love to travel. My big goal is to leave a legacy of drastic steppers who act and are always DRASTIC!

Join a Network in Action Global Partners Group

As you can see, our community is not your ordinary networking organization. We are a business community that is about supporting one another and helping each other grow beyond referrals. Network in Action International believes that the perfect mix of technology and face-to-face networking will help your business grow. There are 7 key differences why NIA works:

1. Monthly Business Meetings - Monthly meetings versus weekly, saving you over 80 hours a year!
2. Professional Leadership – Our groups are run by a professional community builder and network. What this means is that our members are not responsible to grow the group or spend countless hours volunteering for the organization.
3. Refer with Confidence - We require a background check and business assessment on every member. This assures that you can refer our members into someone's personal space without worry of a criminal background.
4. Technology - Our website and mobile app provide real-time connections plus a video profile in lieu of an elevator pitch; saving 25 minutes at every meeting!
5. Bonus Meetings - Optional monthly national speed networking, sales mastery training and a speaker series that bring together NIA members globally.

6. Community Service - Every group has an opportunity to give back to their community and we offer a free membership to a community non-profit.
7. Guaranteed ROR - No other networking organization offers a return on relationships guarantee, but we do! If you do your part, we will guarantee your results in writing!

Beyond networking we have business growth tools such as a marketing and sales electronic learning library. We also have reputation management software to help our business owners to get reviews on Google and Facebook. We offer Customer Relationship Management software, the opportunity to be an author in a collaboration book and the ability to post blogs on our site.

If you are an entrepreneur who's ready to get known and get connected so that you can build relationships that last a lifetime, contact Toni Harris Taylor, Franchise Owner, 713.387.9273 or Toni@NetworkinAction.com

Become a Network in Action Leader

Owning a Network in Action franchise is one of the best decisions I've ever made for my business. It is so rewarding to see my members connect, collaborate and grow. The bonus is that I get to make money doing what I love. I invite you to look at becoming a leader on my team to grow a community of business owners. This is a part-time income opportunity for the right person. The ideal candidate is a business coach, business consultant, marketing strategist or any business that works with small businesses and is passionate about small business growth. This opportunity is right for those who want to:

- Control your time and income
- Add another complimentary stream of income
- Have a deep desire to help entrepreneurs to connect, grow and stay in business

After only 7 years, NIA has over 75 franchise owners in 20+ states and we continue to grow rapidly. We are also proud to be an award-winning franchise from *Entrepreneur* magazine.

NIA has won awards for:

- 2021 Top New Franchise
- 2021 Fastest Growing Franchises
- 2021 Top Part-Time Franchise
- 2022 Best of the Best Franchise
- 2022 Top Home-Based Franchise
- 2022 Top Low-Cost Franchise

If you would like to explore owning your own NIA franchise, contact:

Toni@NetworkinAction.com or 713.387.9273. It's one of the best decisions I've ever made, and it can be for you too!

Made in the USA
Middletown, DE
25 April 2023